EXPLORING
THE TEXTURE
OF TEXTS

Exploring THE Texture OF Texts

A GUIDE TO
SOCIO-RHETORICAL
INTERPRETATION

Vernon K. Robbins

TRINITY PRESS INTERNATIONAL
Valley Forge, Pennsylvania

Trinity Press International, P.O. Box 851, Valley Forge, PA 19482-0851

Library of Congress Cataloging-in-Publication Data

Robbins, Vernon K. (Vernon Kay), 1939-
    Exploring the texture of texts : a guide to socio-rhetorical
interpretations / Vernon K. Robbins.
        p.   cm.
    Includes bibliographical references and indexes.
    ISBN 1-56338-183-4 (alk. paper)
    1. Bible N.T. – Socio-rhetorical criticism. 2. Bible. N.T. –
Criticism, interpretation, etc.   I. Title
BS2380.R62   1996
225.6 – dc20   96-42945
                                                        CIP

Printed in the United States of America

96   97   98   99   10   9   8   7   6   5   4   3   2   1

To all of my students
past, present, and future

Contents

Preface

Fond memories emerge as I recall both the students at Emory University and the people at Central Presbyterian Church in Atlanta who have contributed their enthusiasm to the development of socio-rhetorical interpretation during the past decade. I regret that it is impractical to name the classes, year by year, where students followed guidelines I presented to them for writing multiple interpretations of a text. After the concept of multiple textures emerged during the summer of 1990, the guidelines began to move toward the shape they have in this volume. Finally, by the spring of 1992, both undergraduate and Ph.D. students found it possible to use the guidelines without substantial difficulties. Final revisions and additions during the last four years have been especially pleasant in the context of interaction with people on three different continents. I wish to thank them for their interest, their encouragement, their questions, and their criticisms. Many people, in many different ways, have contributed, and I am grateful.

I would be remiss if I did not mention a few people and institutions in particular. Wesley Wachob and Russell Sisson had the courage to write socio-rhetorical Ph.D. dissertations when the guidelines were still developing. Mary Foskett and Kyle Keefer contributed some specific items to this volume when they revised materials as teaching associates in my class on the New Testament in its context. At the beginning of 1996, Faith Hawkins worked carefully through the manuscript, making both sharp criticisms and helpful suggestions. The final product is much better as a result, and I thank her. I, of course, bear responsibility for the weaknesses that are still present. Gregory Stevenson compiled the indexes with competence and efficiency.

As a result of exceptional kindness and support of my work by a number of people, I was a Visiting Research Scholar during summer 1996 — sponsored by the Centre for Science Development, Human Sciences Research Council — in South Africa, giving lectures and seminars on socio-rhetorical interpretation. I am especially indebted to Dr. Jan Botha for being my primary host and Professor Bernard Combrink for being my cohost at the University of Stellenbosch. Together they issued the invitation, wrote the proposal for the funding, and arranged the schedule for lectures and seminars. I also appreciate the kind welcome of Asa Maree-Snijders of the center when I visited her in Pretoria.

In addition, I must thank Johan Thom, Bernard Lategan, Pieter Coertzen, Charles Wanamaker, Douglas Lawrie, Elna Mouton, Lionel Hendricks, Japi

Havemann, Martin Oosthuisen, Johannes Vorster, Pieter Craffert, Johannes Eugene Botha, Pieter J. J. Botha, Fika van Rensburg, Elma Cornelius, Lilly Nortjé, Hendrik Viviers, and Jan du Rand for their hard work, hospitality, and kindness on behalf of me and my wife, Deanna. There are many others, whose names are not here, who offered hospitality, stimulating conversation, and encouragement, for which I always shall be grateful.

Last of all, I wish to thank Hal Rast for his enthusiasm about this book and Hank Schlau for his excellent copyediting.

The New Approach Called Socio-Rhetorical Criticism

Socio-rhetorical criticism is an approach to literature that focuses on values, convictions, and beliefs both in the texts we read and in the world in which we live (Robbins 1994d, 1995a, 1996). The approach invites detailed attention to the text itself. In addition, it moves interactively into the world of the people who wrote the texts and into our present world. At the outset, it may be helpful to explain each part of the term "socio-rhetorical."

The Meaning of "Socio-Rhetorical"

The hyphenated prefix "socio-" refers to the rich resources of modern anthropology and sociology that socio-rhetorical criticism brings to the interpretation of a text. Social-scientific approaches — which study social class, social systems, personal and community status, people on the margins, and people in positions of power — have become more and more common and important during the last half of the twentieth century (Malina 1993; Elliott 1986, 1993). Socio-rhetorical interpretation brings the ever growing insights of such modes of interpretation into practices of intricate, detailed exegesis of texts.

The term "rhetorical" refers to the way language in a text is a means of communication among people. Rhetorical analysis and interpretation give special attention to the subjects and topics a text uses to present thought, speech, stories, and arguments (Mack 1990). People use language to establish friendships, to set certain people off as enemies, to negotiate with the kinspeople among whom they live, to pursue their self-interests, and to create a view of the world that offers a sense of security and a vision of greater things to be achieved both in this life and after it. Thus, socio-rhetorical criticism integrates the ways people use language with the ways they live in the world.

One of the most notable contributions of socio-rhetorical criticism is to bring literary criticism (Petersen 1978; Powell 1990), social-scientific criticism, rhetorical criticism (Watson and Hauser 1994), postmodern criticism

(Moore 1992, 1994; Adam 1995), and theological criticism (Schneiders 1991) together into an integrated approach to interpretation. These methods have appeared in the creative, fruitful environment of national and international biblical interpretation during the last twenty-five years. Each method has great strengths, but when interpreters use only one of them, the result is too limited. When an interpreter uses them interactively, a rich and responsible approach is available for dealing with belief, action, and life in the world today. No interpreter will ever use all of the resources of socio-rhetorical criticism in any one interpretation. But no interpreter ever uses all of the resources of any method in an interpretation. The purpose is to build an environment for interpretation that provides interpreters with a basic, overall view of life as we know it and language as we use it. Within this environment, interpreters can decide to work especially energetically on one or two aspects of a text. All the time, however, interpreters must hold in view the relation of what they are doing to what other interpreters are doing. Also, they will understand that any analysis and interpretation of a text yield highly limited insight into this text. No complete interpretation of a text is humanly possible, and this state of things should be admitted as one begins the exciting task of interpretation.

A major challenge of socio-rhetorical criticism, then, is to bring practices of interpretation together that often are separated from one another. The separation exists not only among different disciplines of study but also between systematic methods of analysis and skills people use on a daily basis in their lives. The task is to integrate skills people use in ordinary life with exploration of the intricacies of the language in a text. In other words, interpretation is guided by the insight that language is a means of negotiating meanings in and among the worlds in which people live. This means interpreters are also asked to become aware of their own social location and personal interests as they attempt to approach the social location and personal interests the text embodies. This is a large task in an environment of systematic interpretation, but it is a challenge many people negotiate with significant skill in the routine of their daily lives. The goal of socio-rhetorical interpretation is to bring skills we use on a daily basis into an environment of interpretation that is both intricately sensitive to detail and perceptively attentive to large fields of meanings in the world in which we live.

Multiple Textures in a Text

In order to achieve the goals described thus far, socio-rhetorical criticism approaches the text as though it were a thickly textured tapestry (Robbins 1996). Like an intricately woven tapestry, a text contains complex patterns and images. Looked at only one way, a text exhibits a very limited range of its texture. By changing the interpreter's angle a number of times, the method enables the interpreter to bring multiple textures of the text into view. In this book, socio-rhetorical criticism exhibits five different angles to explore multiple textures within texts: (*a*) inner texture; (*b*) inter-texture; (*c*) social and cultural texture; (*d*) ideological texture; and (*e*) sacred texture.

Inner texture concerns features like the repetition of particular words, the creation of beginnings and endings, alternation of speech and storytelling, particular ways in which the words present arguments, and the particular "feel" or aesthetic of the text. Literary and rhetorical criticism often focus on these aspects of a text in distinctive ways. Socio-rhetorical criticism brings both literary and rhetorical techniques together to analyze aspects of words and meanings in the text.

Intertexture concerns a text's configuration of phenomena that lie out-side the text. Oral-scribal intertexture concerns the specific use of language in other texts and people's use of language in daily speech. Social inter-texture concerns phenomena like the clothes people wear, the structure of families and households, political arrangements, military activities, and distri-bution of food, money, and services. Cultural intertexture concerns modes of understanding and belief, like the ideas people have about their importance, their opportunities, and their responsibilities in the world. Historical inter-texture concerns events that occur outside of texts and become historical accounts by means of narrative discourse. As interpreters explore the inter-texture of a text, then, they are continually looking at phenomena outside and inside the text being interpreted. In a context of comparison, the text's particular configuration of phenomena in the world takes on a richer, thicker quality.

Social and cultural texture — not to be confused with social and cultural *inter*texture — concerns the capacities of the text to support social reform, withdrawal, or opposition and to evoke cultural perceptions of dominance, subordinance, difference, or exclusion. Specific social topics in the text ex-hibit resources for changing people or social practices, for destroying and re-creating social order, for withdrawing from present society to create one's own social world, or for coping with the world by transforming one's own perceptions of it. Common social and cultural topics in the discourse deepen the interpreter's understanding of the range of customary practices, central values, modes of relationship and exchange, perceptions about resources for life and well-being, and presuppositions about purity and taboo the text em-bodies. Final cultural categories in the text exhibit the range of values and practices it selects for emphasis and the priority it establishes among them. The priority certain people give to the right, lawful, expedient, honorable, pleasant, easy, feasible, necessary, holy, and so on, produces a particular social and cultural location for them. The result of these locations is the establish-ment of dominant, subordinate, oppositional, and marginal cultures within any locale or region. Analysis and interpretation of the social and cultural texture of a text, then, explore the range of social orientation and locations in the discourse and the manner in which it relates these orientations and locations to one another.

Ideological texture concerns particular alliances and conflicts the language in a text and the language in an interpretation evoke and nurture. Ideological texture concerns the way the text itself and interpreters of the text position themselves in relation to other individuals and groups. Ideological texture differs from social and cultural texture by the manner in which it extends beyond social and cultural location into particular ways in which people advance their own interests and well-being through action, emotion, and thought. The issue is not simply "how" the language of the text and of the interpretation of a text aligns itself with or against other individuals and groups. The issue is the nature of the "particular view itself" that the language evokes and nurtures. Since different modes of intellectual discourse evoke different ways of viewing people and reality, every particular mode of interpretation has its own range of ideological texture. Thus, significantly different ideological ranges of texture exist in anthropological, feminist, theological, literary, or historical modes of interpretive discourse. Interpretive discourse itself, then, takes an interpreter into ideological issues concerning the nature of text itself, the manner in which a text may evoke different points of view, the nature of interpretation, and the nature of the relation of any one interpreter to other interpreters.

Sacred texture exists in texts that somehow address the relation of humans to the divine. Biblical texts certainly contain sacred texture, but they vary from one another in the kind of sacred texture they possess. Many texts other than the Bible and scriptures of other religious traditions contain sacred texture. Sacred texture exists in communication about gods, holy persons, spirit beings, divine history, human redemption, human commitment, religious community, and ethics. Analysis of sacred texture is a way of systematically probing dynamics across a spectrum of relationships between the human and the divine.

In summary, socio-rhetorical criticism challenges interpreters to explore a text in a systematic, plentiful environment of interpretation and dialogue. Underlying the method is a presupposition that words themselves work in complex ways to communicate meanings that we only partially understand. It also presupposes that meanings themselves have their meanings by their relation to other meanings. In other words, all of our attempts to name truth are limited insights into small aspects of the relation of things and meanings to one another. Interpreters and investigators have acquired amazing abilities, however, to describe the relation of things and meanings in complex but structured ways that are informative about life and the world in which we live. Socio-rhetorical criticism challenges interpreters to use a wide spectrum of these amazing human abilities when they investigate and interpret biblical texts.

Ways to Use This Book

There are various ways a person may wish to begin using this book. There is no requirement that a person follow the order in which the book presents the textures. People interpreting biblical or other explicitly religious texts may wish to begin by analyzing the sacred texture of a particular text, a form of analysis discussed in chapter 5. Since there is so much analysis of sacred texture in commentaries and articles available both to scholars and to students, chapter 5 contains no bibliographical references. It is advisable for people who start with that chapter to work interactively with past and current interpretive literature as they analyze and interpret the sacred texture of a text. After an initial analysis of sacred texture, the interpreter may thicken and deepen the interpretation with analysis of aspects of two or three other textures.

Another way is to begin with the inner texture of a text, the subject of chapter 1. For two reasons, socio-rhetorical criticism was created by working from inner texture to intertexture, social and cultural texture, ideological texture, and sacred texture (see Robbins 1992a, 1994d). First, since the nineteenth century certainly, and in some circles earlier, there has been an emphasis on "exegesis" of biblical texts (the discipline of reading "out from" a text what is in it) rather than "eisegesis" (a practice of reading "into" a text what a person wishes to see there). Beginning with the inner texture of a text is a way of trying to gain complex and intricate knowledge of the wording, phrasing, imagery, aesthetics, and argumentative quality of the text. Second, the emergence of modern literary criticism of the Bible during the past quarter of a century has brought an emphasis on "the world of the text itself." Analysis of inner texture is a way of merging literary approaches that are attentive to all kinds of aspects of "the text itself" with an emphasis on "exegesis," reading out from the text what is in it. Interpreters who place a high priority on either or both of these aspects of biblical texts may find it most rewarding to work first with inner texture and then to move on to other textures of the text.

People with special interest in historical criticism may wish to start with the intertexture of a text, the subject of chapter 2. As historical critics interpret a text, they always have their eye on some historically accessible phenomena outside the text. Intertextual analysis, then, lies at the base of their interests. Again, once an interpreter performs an intertextual analysis, it is important to broaden the analysis and interpretation through attention to at least two other textures of the text.

A person may wish to begin with the social and cultural texture of the text (chap. 3). Especially interpreters who emphasize a sharp difference between ancient and modern society may wish to begin here. Social-scientific critics, who emphasize the evils of ethnocentricity and anachronism, consider the social and cultural texture of the text to be the most important mode of entry for North American and northern European interpreters. Again, it is important for interpreters to work significantly with at least two other textures in addition to its social and cultural texture to deepen the analysis and interpretation of the text.

Still another way is for a person to begin with ideological texture (chap. 4). A major reason for this may be a perception that an ideology generates every text and every interpretation. People who like the excitement of conflict or consider conflict to be the most productive mode of activity in the world may wish to set alternative texts and alternative interpretations against one another as a beginning point for interpretation. Again, it is important for an interpreter to deepen this beginning point with analysis and interpretation of at least two other textures of the text. The interplay among these textures initiates a dialogical environment among multiple modes of perceiving a text and multiple modes for a text to function within the lives of people.

Chapter 1

Inner Texture

GETTING INSIDE A TEXT

The inner texture of a text resides in features in the language of the text itself, like repetition of words and use of dialogue between two persons to communicate the information. In other words, inner texture is the texture of the medium of communication. With written texts, the inner texture especially resides in verbal texture — the texture of the language itself.

Inner textual analysis focuses on words as tools for communication. This is a stage of analysis prior to analysis of "meanings," that is, prior to "real interpretation" of the text. Sometimes it helps for the interpreter to "remove all meanings" from the words and simply look at and listen to "the words themselves" to perform this analysis. This analysis works only with a basic sense of the words. The analyst looks at and listens to the ways in which the text uses these words (e.g., repetition of the same word many times, statement of almost the same thing in many different ways, careful sequencing of new terms that build to a strong conclusion, etc.). The purpose of this analysis is to gain an intimate knowledge of words, word patterns, voices, structures, devices, and modes in the text, which are the context for meanings and meaning-effects that an interpreter analyzes with the other readings of the text.

To move toward a goal of teaching inner textual analysis to the reader, this chapter identifies and enacts six kinds of inner texture in a text: (a) repetitive; (b) progressive; (c) narrational; (d) opening-middle-closing; (e) argumentative; and (f) sensory-aesthetic texture. The chapter exhibits these kinds of inner texture in Mark 15:1–16:8. In this instance, then, the analysis focuses on narrative discourse in the New Testament — discourse that tells a story. Readers who are interested in inner textual analysis of epistolary discourse in the New Testament may consult another of my publications (Robbins 1996).

When interpreters focus closely on a text, they work with inner textures of the text even if they are not conscious that this is what they are doing. An interpreter may begin with any of these inner textures, but for many people it will be better to learn how to analyze each aspect of inner texture in the order in which they appear in this chapter. Only very few interpreters, however advanced, will find the commitment, interest, or ability to perform all of these strategies of analysis on one text in a sequence. It is advisable, therefore, that a person, after reading through the analyses of Mark 15:1–16:8 in this chapter, experiment with three or four of the strategies of analysis on a particular span of text and select those that work most readily with it.

A. Repetitive Texture and Pattern

Repetitive texture resides in the occurrence of words and phrases more than once in a unit. When the same word occurs at least twice in a text, the result is repetition. Multiple occurrences of many different kinds of grammatical, syntactical, verbal, or topical phenomena may produce repetitive texture. Sometimes repetition occurs in topics like resurrection, suffering, and hope; sometimes in pronouns like "I," "you," and "we"; sometimes in negatives like "no," "not," and "no one"; sometimes in conjunctions or adverbs like "then," "but," "because," and so on. Patterns of repetition appear most clearly when the interpreter first marks the repeated words somehow in the text itself, then exhibits them in some kind of systematic diagram (Robbins 1994d, 1996).

Repetition that exhibits major characters and major topics in the discourse in Mark 15:1–16:8 creates the pattern shown in table 1. This table shows that Jesus is a subject of central interest throughout Mark 15:1–16:8. In this context, nine references to Pilate and seven references to king or kingdom occur in 15:1–44. Eight references to crucifixion occur in 15:13–32; then an additional reference occurs in 16:6. Three references to women begin in 15:40 and extend through 16:1. Six references to a tomb begin in 15:45 and continue to the very end in 16:8. This clustering of repetitive data creates three major sets of rhetorical topics. First, there is repetition that features Jesus, Pilate, and kingship. Second, there is repetition that features crucifixion. Third, there is repetition of references to three women, Joseph of Arimathea, and Pilate that shifts the focus to a tomb that is empty in the final scene.

The repetitive texture of a span of text regularly exhibits initial glimpses into the overall rhetorical movements in the discourse. Repetition does not reveal the precise nature of the boundaries between one unit and another. Also, repetition does not exhibit inner meanings in the sequences. But repetitive texture introduces interpreters to the overall forest, if you will, so they know where they are as they look at individual trees. Clusters of repetitive data give initial insight into the overall picture of the discourse. They provide an overarching view of the texture of the language that invites the interpreter to move yet closer to the details of the text.

Table 1
PROGRESSION OF PEOPLE AND TOPICS IN MARK 15:1–16:8

Verse	Jesus	Pilate	king	crucify	cross	Mary	Joseph	tomb
1:	Jesus	Pilate						
2:		Pilate	king					
4:		Pilate						
5:	Jesus	Pilate						
8:		Pilate						
9:			king					
12:		Pilate	king					
13:				crucify				
14:				crucify				
15:	Jesus	Pilate		crucified				
18:			king					
20:				crucify				
21:					cross			
24:				crucified				
25:				crucified				
26:			king					
27:				crucified				
30:					cross			
32:			king	crucified	cross			
34:	Jesus							
40:						Mary M.; Mary; Salome		
43:	Jesus	Pilate	kingdom				Joseph	
44:		Pilate						
45:							Joseph	
46:								tomb
								tomb
47:						Mary M.; Mary		
16:1						Mary M.; Mary; Salome		
16:2								tomb
16:3								tomb
16:5								tomb
16:6	Jesus			crucified				
16:8								tomb

B. Progressive Texture and Pattern

Progressive texture resides in sequences (progressions) of words and phrases throughout the unit. Sometimes words alternate with one another throughout the unit, like "I...you," "now...then," "because...therefore," "good... bad"; sometimes words form a sequence of steps like "I, I, I...they, they... we, we, us"; sometimes words form a chain like "hope and righteousness... righteousness and God...God and people who believe." Again, sequential patterns appear most clearly when an interpreter first marks them somehow in the text itself, then exhibits them in a systematic diagram.

Progression emerges out of repetition. Indeed, repetition itself is one kind of progression, since movement from the first occurrence of a word to another occurrence is a forward movement — a progression — in the discourse. Focusing on progression within repetition adds more dimensions to the analysis. First, it may lead to observations about progressive texture in the entire work. Second, it may exhibit phenomena that function as stepping stones to other phenomena in the text. Third, it may exhibit a sequence of subunits throughout a span of text.

An interpreter experiences significant limitations on a printed page when displaying progressive texture because all the words in a text present its progression. A diagram containing all the words of a text, obviously, is too full to call attention to special progressive phenomena in it. Since repeated items especially are the building stones for progressions, it is good to build a progressive diagram on certain repeated items in the text.

One very intriguing progression in Mark 15:1–16:8 occurs in language about kingship. In the context of repetition concerning Jesus, Pilate, crucifixion, and Joseph of Arimathea, this progression looks as is shown in table 2.

Table 2
KINGSHIP PROGRESSION IN MARK 15:1–16:8

1:	Jesus	Pilate			
2:		Pilate	King of the Jews		
4:		Pilate			
5:	Jesus	Pilate			
8:		Pilate			
9:			King of the Jews		
12:		Pilate	King of the Jews		
13:				crucify	
14:				crucify	
15:	Jesus	Pilate		crucified	
18:			King of the Jews		
20:				crucify	
24:				crucified	
25:				crucified	
26:			King of the Jews		
27:				crucified	
32:			*Messiah King of Israel*	crucified	
34:	Jesus				
43:	Jesus	Pilate	*kingdom of God*		Joseph
44:		Pilate			Joseph
16:6	Jesus			crucified	

This display reveals a progression from "King of the Jews" to "crucifixion" to "Messiah King of Israel" to "kingdom of God." The question is what this progression might mean, and for this it can help to turn to progressive texture in the entire text. Progression of all the phrases concerning kingship produces the following list:

1:15	kingdom of God
3:24	kingdom divided against itself
4:11	kingdom of God
4:26	kingdom of God
4:30	kingdom of God
6:14	King Herod
6:22	king
6:23	my (Herod's) kingdom
6:25	king
6:26	king
6:27	king
9:1	kingdom of God
9:47	kingdom of God
10:14	kingdom of God
10:15	kingdom of God
10:23	kingdom of God
10:24	kingdom of God
10:25	kingdom of God
11:10	kingdom of our father David
12:34	kingdom of God
13:8	kingdom of God
13:9	kings
14:25	kingdom of God
15:2	King of the Jews
15:9	King of the Jews
15:12	King of the Jews
15:18	King of the Jews
15:26	King of the Jews
15:32	Messiah King of Israel
15:43	kingdom of God

This list shows that the kingdom of God is a topic within the repetitive texture of the Gospel of Mark. It also reveals a general reference to kingdoms in 3:24, specific references to King Herod and his kingdom in 6:14–27, and reference to the kingdom of our father David in 11:10. The progression from

King of the Jews to Messiah King of Israel to kingdom of God in the account of Jesus' crucifixion, burial, and resurrection, then, occurs in a broader progressive context concerning kingdom and kingship in the Gospel of Mark.

What is the significance of this aspect of progressive texture in Mark? Certainly the crucifixion, death, and resurrection of Jesus are related to the coming of the kingdom of God. Will the kingdom come after the death and resurrection of Jesus? Are the death and resurrection the beginning of the kingdom of God, or did the kingdom already begin during the activity of Jesus (1:15)? It appears that the kingdom begins to arrive with Jesus' activity and will fully arrive when Jesus returns as Son of man (9:1; 13:26). But there is another issue. Pilate speaks of Jesus as King of the Jews, and chief priests and scribes refer to him as Messiah King of Israel. What is the relation of Jesus' kingship to the kingship of others in the Mediterranean world? Investigation of this issue requires analysis of texts outside the Gospel of Mark. Therefore, this issue will become important in the next chapter, which concerns intertexture rather than inner texture. As indicated above, analysis of inner texture is a limited form of analysis. It is necessary to supplement inner textual analysis with other forms of analysis to address issues like the meaning of Jesus' kingship in the context of perceptions about kingship in the first-century Mediterranean world in which the Gospel of Mark was written.

Another aspect of progressive texture in Mark 15:1–16:8 occurs around seeing, as is shown in table 3. When Jesus is handed over to Pilate, the chief priests accuse Jesus of many things (15:3). When Jesus does not reply to their charges, Pilate says to him, "See how many charges they bring against you" (15:4). When Pilate sees the insistence of the chief priests and the crowd, he finally gives in to their wish for Jesus to be crucified. When Jesus is on the cross, chief priests and scribes raise the issue of what they are able to "see." If Jesus will only come down from the cross, they say, they will be able to see and believe that he is the Messiah. The topic of seeing continues when the centurion standing opposite Jesus sees Jesus die and asserts that Jesus truly is son of God. The emphasis on seeing progresses to a sequence of observing by the women. Standing afar, they observe both the death of Jesus and the tomb where Joseph lays him for burial. When they go to the tomb on the morning after the sabbath, they observe the stone rolled back and they see a young man who speaks to them. In turn, the man tells them the disciples will see Jesus in Galilee. Seeing, then, is a topic that moves the narrative forward from the accusations against Jesus to the taunting of him on the cross to his death, burial, and resurrection. Seeing in Mark is such an extensive topic that it cannot be pursued in detail here. One of the key questions is whether the disciples are to see the resurrected Jesus or Jesus as the returned Son of man in Galilee (16:7). Another issue is the relation of sight to the other senses: hearing, touching, tasting, and smelling. We will return briefly to sight in the section on sensory-aesthetic texture below. Seeing is an important part of the progressive texture of the account of Jesus' death and resurrection in Mark.

Table 3
PROGRESSION OF SEEING IN MARK 15:1–16:8

3:	accused				
4:	accused	see			
13:			crucify		
14:			crucify		
15:			to be crucified		
20:			crucify		
24:			crucified		
25:			crucified		
27:			crucified		
32:		may see	crucified with		
35:		see			
36:		may see			
39:		seeing			
40:				observed	
46:					tomb
					tomb
47:				observed	
16:2					tomb
16:3					tomb
16:4		looking up		observe	
16:5		saw			tomb
16:6		see	crucified		
16:7		will see			
16:8					tomb

A still more detailed analysis of progressive texture in Mark 15:1–16:8 reveals a sequence of seven scenes (see table 4). These scenes emerge from a reading of the text that is attentive to exceptionally brief patterns of repetition and progression. Embedded in the larger patterns that come into view with the initial analysis of repetitive and progressive texture, these brief patterns reveal an intricately configured environment of actions and responses that move the narrative forward from the delivery of Jesus to Pilate to Jesus' absence from a tomb. Table 4 was generated through highly detailed analysis of repetitive and progressive phenomena in the Greek text (Robbins 1992b). Some of the items are difficult to see in English translation because the English words may not repeat the same words and word stems. Only this kind of close analysis, however, can produce a detailed outline of the scenes in the story. The major reason for presenting this table is to provide the opportunity to make observations about specific scenes throughout Mark 15:1–16:8 in the remainder of this book.

Table 4

SCENES BASED ON REPETITIVE AND PROGRESSIVE TEXTURE

1. Mark 15:1–15: Selection of Jesus to Be Humiliated and Crucified

1:	delivered	bound (*dēsantes*)			
6:		prisoner (*desmion*)	released		
7:		in prison (*dedemenos*)			
9:			release		
10:	delivered				
11:			release		
13:				cried out	crucify
14:				cried out	crucify
15:	delivered		released		to be crucified

2. Mark 15:16–24: Mockery of Jesus as Royalty

16:	led him away			
17:		clothed	purple cloak	
20:	led him out to crucify him	unclothed	purple cloak	
		clothed		his garments
24:	and they crucified him	divided		his garments

3. Mark 15:25–32: Jesus Hangs on the Cross

25:	they crucified him
27:	they crucified with him
32:	those crucified with him

4. Mark 15:33–39: Jesus' Crying Out and Death

34:	loud cry	Eloi, Eloi		
35:	cries out	Elijah	bystanders	see
36:		Elijah		see if
37:	loud cry			breathed his last
39:			bystander	seeing breathed his last

5. Mark 15:40–41: Women Observe the Crucifixion of Jesus

40:	women	observed					
41:			Galilee	followed	served	went up	Jerusalem

6. Mark 15:42–46: Permission for and Burial of Jesus' Corpse

43:	Joseph					
		Pilate	body			
44:		Pilate		dead		
				dead	centurion	
45:	Joseph		corpse		centurion	
46:						tomb
						tomb

7. Mark 15:47–16:8: Women Visit the Empty Tomb

47:	observed	laid			
16:1			sabbath		
16:2			sabbath	tomb	
16:3				tomb	stone
16:4	observed				stone
16:5				tomb	amazed
16:6		laid			amazed
16:7				tomb	

C. Narrational Texture and Pattern

Narrational texture resides in voices (often not identified with a specific character) through which the words in texts speak. The opening words in a
text automatically presuppose a narrator speaking the words. The narrator
may begin and continue simply with "narration"; the narrator may introduce
people (characters) who act (the narrator describes their action); the narrator may introduce people who speak (they themselves become "narrators" or
"speaking actors"); the narrator may introduce "written texts" that speak (like
Old Testament scripture). Usually the narrational texture reveals some kind
of pattern that moves the discourse programmatically forward. Sometimes a
pattern emerges when narration and attributed speech alternate with each
other. Sometimes a particular type of speech, like a question or a command,
occurs so frequently that it establishes a narrational pattern in the discourse.
Narrational patterns regularly give the interpreter a closer look at the units
or scenes in the discourse.

In Mark 15:1–16:8, only one scene (15:40–41) contains narration without
attributed or reported speech. The remaining six scenes alternate narrational
discourse with direct or reported speech. In the first scene (Mark 15:1–15),
nine verses are entirely narration and the discourse attributes speech to Pilate
five times, to Jesus twice (15:2, 4), and to the crowd three times (15:9, 12,
14). All five times Pilate speaks, he asks questions:

a. Are you the King of the Jews? (15:2)

b. Have you no answer to make? (15:4)

c. Do you want me to release for you the King of the Jews? (15:9)

d. Then what shall I do with the man whom you call the King of the Jews?
(15:12)

e. Why, what evil has he done? (15:14)

This sequence of questions introduces a definition of Jesus as "king" that
reverberates through the unit to its end. In addition, this sequence evokes a
view of Pilate as an intermediary who simply asks for information and acts
on the basis of that information. Viewing the questions on their own reveals
two subscenes (15:2–5, 6–15). First, Pilate's questions to Jesus evoke alarm
in Pilate when Jesus has no answer to make to charges against him. Second,
Pilate's questions to the crowd evoke exasperation in Pilate when they want
to crucify a man whom he has called king and who has done no evil.

Through questions, then, narrational discourse initially attributes the definition of Jesus as a king to a Roman, Pilate; not to a Jew of any kind — like
a chief priest, scribe, elder, Pharisee, or Sadducee. In the context of Pilate's
third articulation of the title "the King of the Jews," the Jerusalem crowd introduces the concept of crucifying Jesus. The formulation of the question in

terms of "whom *you* call King of the Jews" is a decisive narrational feature since no Jew or Jerusalemite has called Jesus king, yet Pilate asserts that this is the name they give him. In the context of a Roman evoking the title "king" for Jesus and the crowd's insistence that Pilate crucify him, the unit ends with the narrational comment that Pilate "agreed" to carry out the crucifixion.

The narrational discourse in the second major scene (15:16–24) presents only one instance of attributed speech:

And they [the soldiers] began to salute him, "Hail, King of the Jews!" (15:18)

In this scene, then, a key feature is the transmission of the concept of king from Pilate to the soldiers who carry out the crucifixion. The narrative context characterizes the speech and action of the soldiers as a mockery of Jesus as a king. This sets the stage for the crucifixion as a mockery of Jesus' speech and action in the entire Gospel of Mark.

The discourse in the third scene (15:25–32) contains extended speech attributed to passersby, chief priests, and scribes, which will be discussed below in the section on oral-scribal intertexture. This section perpetuates the topic of kingship first through narrational commentary:

And the inscription of the charge against him read, "The King of the Jews." (15:26)

After this commentary, direct discourse attributed to the chief priests with the scribes defines the topic of kingship from the perspective of Jewish speakers:

Let the Messiah, the King of Israel, come down from the cross, that we may see and believe. (15:32)

In the context of the narrational discourse and the speech attributed to the chief priests and scribes about Jesus and kingship, narrational discourse identifies the two men who were crucified with Jesus as bandits or revolutionaries (15:27).

The discourse in the fourth scene (15:33–39) introduces five statements, with the initial statement by Jesus providing the context for the four that come after it:

a. Jesus: Eloi, Eloi, lama sabachthani?

b. Narrator: Which means, "My God, my God, why hast thou forsaken me?"

c. Bystanders: Behold, he is calling Elijah.

d. Bystander: Wait, let us see whether Elijah will come to take him down.

e. Centurion: Truly this man was son of God.

The importance of this sequence heightens when we place it in the context of the progressive texture analyzed above. The opening of Mark 15 features Pilate asking two questions to Jesus: (a) "Are you King of the Jews?"; and (b) "Have you no answer to make? See how many charges they make against you." Jesus acknowledges Pilate's statement with "You have said so" (15:2), but he makes no answer to the charges of the chief priests. This establishes a mode in which Jesus responds to no one until the scene of his death. When Jesus finally does speak, he speaks not to people but to God. The result is that bystanders mock him by either pretending or misunderstanding that "Eloi" refers to Elijah. All-knowing narrational commentary tells the reader that Jesus' cry means "My God, my God, why have you forsaken me?" The centurion, in contrast to the bystanders, responds not with a misunderstanding of "Eloi" but with a perception that Jesus has a special relation to God. This establishes a sequence in the narrative as follows:

Pilate: "King of the Jews"
Soldiers: "King of the Jews"
Inscription on the cross: "King of the Jews"
Chief priests with scribes: "Messiah King of Israel"
Centurion: "son of God"

The concept of "kingship" that the Roman procurator introduced in the initial scene is reconfigured to "messiahship" by officials of the Jerusalem temple. Then a Roman centurion — an official in charge of a hundred other soldiers and who likely had participated in the earlier mockery of Jesus as "King of the Jews" — testifies that Jesus is "truly son of God." Narrational texture, then, moves us beyond titles containing the term "king" to the title "son of God." A special topic of interest in the chapter on intertexture will be the relation of kingship to sonship of a god.

The discourse in the fifth scene (Mark 15:40–41) is entirely narration. The narration describes women looking on from afar who have followed Jesus all the way from Galilee and ministered to him. With this move, the all-controlling narrator creates a transition from the cross to a tomb that is empty in the final scene.

The discourse in the sixth scene (Mark 15:42–46) contains reported speech in the context of narration. The narrator remains in charge by defining the day of Jesus' crucifixion and burial as the day of preparation for the sabbath. Then the narrator defines Joseph of Arimathea as an upstanding Jewish person who expects the kingdom of God, and the narrator describes Joseph's approach to Pilate and Pilate's granting of Joseph's request to take Jesus' body down from the cross and to lay it in a tomb. In contrast to the other five scenes in Mark 15:1–16:8, the narrator does not attribute direct speech to the women, to Joseph, or to Pilate in 15:40–46. Rather than allowing characters to become media of direct speech, narrative voice maintains control through description and reporting. In the chapter on intertexture, we will probe more deeply into narration that attributes speech to specific characters and narration in which the narrator maintains control of the speaking voice in the narration. While analysis of narrational texture brings this phenomenon into view, analysis of intertexture creates a context for exploring its deeper meanings and meaning-effects.

The discourse in the seventh scene (Mark 15:47–16:8) begins with narration. After the first three verses, however, the discourse introduces a question by the women:

Who will roll away the stone for us from the door of the tomb?

After two more verses of narration the discourse introduces two verses of extended speech by the young man in the tomb in a white robe:

Do not be amazed.
You seek Jesus of Nazareth, who was crucified.
He has risen; he is not here.
But go, tell the disciples and Peter
that he is going before you to Galilee.
There you will see him, as he told you.

The text ends with narrational discourse that describes the women's flight from the tomb, their amazement, and their absence of speech about it to anyone because of their fear.

In summary, the narrational texture of Mark 15:1–16:8 reveals that throughout the ordeal of Jesus' death, no one says a kind word to him, nor does Jesus say anything redeeming to anyone. People impose humiliation and brutality on Jesus, and in the end he dies crying out to God and is buried by a person anticipating the kingdom of God. Only a Roman centurion recognizes the implications of the ordeal and characterizes Jesus with language that asserts a special relation of Jesus to God. Women who had accompanied Jesus from Galilee watch from a distance as Joseph of Arimathea places his corpse in a tomb. Later, when the women go to the tomb to anoint Jesus' body, they find an open tomb with a young man dressed in a white robe sitting in it. This young man tells them Jesus has risen.

Analysis of narrational texture, then, takes an interpreter into yet more of the data of the discourse. Narrational commentary regularly sets the stage for attributed speech. The alternation of narrational commentary and speech attributed to various characters in the story begins to reveal some of the inner nuances of the story itself. At this point, however, the story may still look "innocent." It may appear that the narrational voice is simply presenting a straightforward account of the way things happened. Yet the narrational texture reveals that there is considerable staging of events in the discourse. The discourse allows only a limited number of people to be on stage. Even among those on stage, only some are allowed to speak. Sometimes the discourse presents the speech of certain people as simply part of "one voice" that a whole group of people speak. The discourse does not allow some people either to speak for themselves or to have a voice at all, even if they are present. In addition, there are many people whom the discourse does not even see.

In Mark, the narrational discourse shifts dramatically near the end to three women who had been observing all the time. In contrast to the previous scenes, this scene contains no direct or reported speech (15:40–41). How many other people, and who, were also watching and participating? And what, one might wonder, did they see that this narrational voice does not see? The next scene (15:42–46) contains reported speech but no direct speech. What is the effect of the narrator's dominance at this point in the story? Among other things, the reader becomes aware that this story presents a particular point of view of these events. We need, then, to look even more closely at the discourse. Let us look next at the opening-middle-closing texture of the Markan account, since an opening, a middle, and a closing are natural parts of a dramatic presentation.

D. Opening-Middle-Closing Texture and Pattern

Opening-middle-closing texture resides in the nature of the beginning, body, and conclusion of a section of discourse. Repetition, progression, and narration regularly work together to create the opening, middle, and closing of a unit of text. For a particular span of narrative text, interpreters often have different views concerning the exact place where the opening ends, where the middle begins and ends, and where the conclusion begins and ends. Often interpreters refine and improve their analysis when they see parts of a complex pattern they did not see in their initial analysis. They may, however, identify phenomena that support a view of units in the narrative that is different from the view of another interpreter. This kind of variation shows how complex opening-middle-closing texture may be. The opening itself may have a beginning, middle, and ending. In addition, the middle may be subdivided in this way, and also the conclusion. Variations may occur because there are different kinds of openings, different kinds of middles, and different kinds of closings. In other words, openings, middles, and closings may have very different kinds of texture.

One of the reasons for selecting Mark 15:1–16:8 is that this span of text has such an interesting opening-middle-closing texture. One of the possibilities, for example, is that some endings really are simply new beginnings. In other words, some endings are really not endings at all. They do not really bring anything to a final conclusion. Rather, some endings simply introduce topics and events that provide resources for a new beginning when everything seemed to be coming to a dramatic, final end. Let us explore some of the opening-middle-closing texture in Mark 15:1–16:8.

The opening scene in Mark 15:1–15 features Jesus being handed over to

Pilate and Pilate asking Jesus if he is King of the Jews. The effect of this scene reaches a conclusion in the death of Jesus on a cross, accompanied by a centurion's assertion that Jesus is son of God (15:33–39). As a result of Markan narration, the crucifixion of Jesus occurs in three steps. First, the soldiers mock Jesus as King of the Jews and hang him on a cross (15:16–24). Second, passersby mock Jesus as the Messiah King of Israel while he hangs on the cross (15:25–32). Third, Jesus dies on the cross, and a centurion declares that he is son of God (15:33–39).

With this sequence, the drama that began with Pilate reaches a dramatic conclusion. Yet the nature of Markan narration, as we already hinted above, may be to present conclusions that simply create contexts for new beginnings. In this instance, the narration introduces women who observed all of the events from afar. The narration says that these women had followed Jesus from Galilee to Jerusalem, serving him (15:40–41). This is a fascinating digression back to the beginning of the story. Just before Jesus entered into Galilee, angels had served him in the wilderness (1:13). When Jesus came into Galilee, four male disciples responded immediately to Jesus' call to follow him (1:16–20). Only now, at the very end of the story, does the narration assert that three women also became followers of Jesus, and they have followed Jesus all the way to Jerusalem.

The women, the narrator tells us, saw Joseph put Jesus' body in the tomb (15:47). Therefore, after the sabbath they return to the tomb to anoint Jesus' body properly with ointments. This leads to a dramatic scene in which the women speak on the way to the tomb, the young man at the tomb makes a lengthy statement to the women while they are in the tomb, and the women flee from the tomb and say nothing to anyone (16:1–8). This means that there are three additional steps after the three steps that present Jesus' crucifixion. In other words, after three scenes that bring Jesus' life to an end (15:16–24, 25–32, 33–39), three more scenes introduce Jesus "going before the disciples to Galilee" (15:40–41, 42–46, 15:47–16:8). By observing the death and burial of Jesus, and by planning a visit to the tomb where Jesus is buried, three women provide a new beginning for a story that had come to a disastrous end. Yet the final scene itself is no real ending. Jesus has gone to Galilee, the young man in a white robe tells the women. Thus, the story goes back to where it began, namely, to Galilee. And the reader already knows that going to Galilee simply means to go to a place where Jesus calls people to follow him. So at the end the story begins all over again. And so it will continue to start again every time a person reads it through to the end.

In summary, three-step narration is a characteristic of storytelling in the Gospel of Mark (Robbins 1981, 1992a), and three-step narration concludes the story. The irony is that this three-step conclusion is simply a step into the future. This future recycles Jesus, his disciples, women who follow him, and the readers of the text back to Galilee, where the initial story began. Analysis of opening-middle-closing texture, then, has taken us into yet other characteristics of the Markan account of Jesus' crucifixion, death, and resurrection.

E. Argumentative Texture and Pattern

Study of argumentative texture investigates multiple kinds of inner reasoning in the discourse. Some of this reasoning is logical. In other words, the discourse presents assertions and supports them with reasons, clarifies them through opposites and contraries, and possibly presents short or elaborate counterarguments. Other reasoning may be described as qualitative. This occurs when the quality of the images and descriptions encourages the reader to accept the portrayal as true and real. This occurs when analogies, examples, and citations of ancient testimony function in a persuasive manner. Rhetorical theory, both ancient and modern, presents extensive analytical tools for analyzing the argumentative texture of texts.

It may be surprising to the reader to suggest that Mark 15:1–16:8 is argumentative. Yet ancient rhetoricians observed that stories as well as speeches used argumentative devices to persuade the reader to think and act in one way rather than another. In the process of their discussions, they identified assertions, reasons, opposites, analogies, examples, and citations of ancient written testimony as the major argumentative devices people use. By the second century B.C.E., they had sorted these devices out — calling them "argumentative topics" — as central to argumentation. An important text from *Rhetorica ad Herennium* (87 B.C.E.) illustrates the centrality of these topics and figures in the argumentation of the time. Citing it in full can ground our insights in discussions contemporary with New Testament literature and introduce us to the rich resources available for analysis of the argumentative texture of literature from antiquity. Once we have explored this quotation, we will be ready to turn to the argumentative texture of Mark 15:1–16:8. *Rhetorica ad Herennium* 4.43.56–44.57 reads as follows:

> The following, then, will illustrate a treatment in seven parts — to continue the use of the same theme for my example, in order that you may know how easily, by the precepts of rhetoric, a simple idea is developed in a multiple manner:
>
> **Thesis**
> "The wise man will, on the republic's behalf, shun no peril,
>
> **Rationales**
> "because it may often happen that if a man has been loath to perish for his country it will be necessary for him to perish with her. Further, since it is from our country that we receive all our advantages, no disadvantage incurred on her behalf is to be regarded as severe.

Contrary with Rationale

"I say, then, that they who flee from the peril to be undergone on behalf of the republic act foolishly, for they cannot avoid the disadvantages, and are found guilty of ingratitude towards the state.

Restatement of Thesis with Rationales

"But on the other hand they who, with peril to themselves, confront the perils of the fatherland, are to be considered wise, since they render to their country the homage due her, and prefer to die for many of their fellow citizens instead of with them. For it is extremely unjust to give back to nature, when she compels, the life you have received from nature, and not to give to your country, when she calls for it, the life you have preserved thanks to your country; and when you can die for fatherland with the greatest manliness and honour, to prefer to live in disgrace and cowardice; and when you are willing to face danger for friends and parents and your other kin, to refuse to run the risk for the republic, which embraces all these and that most holy name of fatherland as well.

Analogy

"He who in a voyage prefers his own to his vessel's security, deserves contempt. No less blameworthy is he who in a crisis of the republic consults his own in preference to the common safety. For from the wreck of a ship many of those on board escape unharmed, but from the wreck of the fatherland no one can swim to safety.

Example and Testimony of Antiquity

"It is this that, in my opinion, Decius well understood, who is said to have devoted himself to death, and, in order to save his legions, to have plunged into the midst of the enemy. He gave up his life, but did not throw it away; for at the cost of a very cheap good he redeemed a sure good, of a small good the greatest good. He gave his life, and received his country in exchange. He lost his life, and gained glory, which, transmitted with highest praise, shines more and more every day as time goes on.

Conclusion

"But if reason has shown and illustration confirmed that it is fitting to confront danger in defence of the republic, they are to be esteemed wise who do not shrink from any peril when the security of the fatherland is at stake." (*Rhetorica ad Herennium* [Cicero] 1954: 4.43.56–44.57)

This text exhibits the importance of thesis, rationale (reason), contrary (or: opposite), analogy, example, and citation of written testimony in argumentation in Mediterranean antiquity. It is especially important at this point to notice the thesis and rationales (or reasons) at the beginning. A thesis and a rationale together make two-thirds of a logical syllogism. In the example from the *Rhetorica ad Herennium* above, the first sentence in the rationale presents the minor premise of the syllogism and the thesis presents the conclusion. When one of the premises is present in the discourse, a reader or hearer is able to supply the missing premise. The full syllogism evoked by the thesis and the first sentence in the rationale produces the following syllogism:

> **[Unstated major premise:** No one wants to perish along with his country.]

> **Minor premise** [rationale]: If a man has been loath to perish for his country, it will be necessary for him to perish with her.

> **Conclusion** [thesis]: (Therefore,) the wise man will, on the republic's behalf, shun no peril.

When these topics and figures appear in narrative, they produce two basic kinds of rhetorical progression: (*a*) logical; and (*b*) qualitative. Logical progression

> has "the form of a perfectly conducted argument, advancing step by step...." As the narrative proceeds, assertions are made that create specific expectations within the reader. Once the reader sees that many of these assertions are fulfilled within a short span of text, he or she expects a logical progression within the text that reliably fulfills all the assertions.... [T]he logic of assertion and fulfillment in Mark has its ultimate source in the logic of promise and fulfillment in biblical literature. In the Gospel of Mark, however, the logic of promise and fulfillment is generalized by allowing assertions both of the narrator and of Jesus to function as powerfully as statements of God or one of his prophets.... Assertions by God, by the narrator, and by Jesus create logical progressions in the narrative as specific expectations are created and fulfilled in the narrative sequence. (Robbins 1992a: 9, quoting Burke 1931: 124)

Qualitative progressions, in contrast to logical progressions,

> occur when an attribute of speech or action, which the reader had no reason to expect on the basis of a previous assertion, emerges in relation to one or more characters in the narrative. When new attributes and new titles emerge in the portrayal of Jesus, the narrative acquires qualitative progressive form. Likewise, when the disciples react differently from what the reader expects, a qualitative rhetorical progression is occurring in the narrative.... In contrast to a logical progression, then, the reader recognizes the appropriateness of the progression only after the events have occurred. (Robbins 1992a: 9–10)

Mark 15:1–15, the first scene of the trial and crucifixion, has a logical progression. The narrational discourse introduces two major syllogisms, one concerning the chief priests and one concerning Pilate:

1. Syllogism concerning the chief priests:

[**Unstated major premise:** When the chief priests were envious of someone, they handed him over to Pilate and stirred the people up to put pressure on Pilate to crucify him.]

Minor premise: The chief priests were envious of Jesus.

Conclusion: Therefore, they handed him over to Pilate and stirred the people up to put pressure on Pilate to crucify him.

2. Syllogism concerning Pilate:

Major premise: Pilate customarily released a prisoner of the people's choice to the people in Jerusalem in honor of their Passover festival.

Minor premise: It was time for the Passover festival in Jerusalem.

Conclusion: The people's choice was Barabbas when Pilate asked them whom they wanted him to release to them.

Narrative discourse, as well as epistolary discourse, regularly states a conclusion first and presents one or both of the premises (reasons) for the conclusion in clauses of rationale ("because" or "for") after the conclusion. Thus, the first syllogistic display above presents information from 15:9 first (the minor premise), then the conclusion which is in 15:1. It is necessary, then, for an interpreter to reverse the order of the discourse when displaying it in syllogistic form. Narrational discourse in the Gospel of Mark openly states the major premise, minor premise, and the conclusion to the syllogism about Pilate. The narration uses the mind of Pilate to convey one part of the minor premise (that the chief priests were envious of Jesus). In addition, narrational address to the implied hearer/reader conveys the other part of the minor premise (that the chief priests stirred up the crowd to have Pilate set Barabbas free and to crucify Jesus). This leaves the major premise unstated (with the certainty that the hearer/reader will construct the conclusion):

Conclusion: The chief priests used the occasion when Pilate released a prisoner to the people at Passover to stir up the crowd to crucify Jesus, whom they envied.

The reader/hearer, then, is asked to trust Pilate (or the narrator's ability to read the mind of Pilate) to know that the chief priests were envious of Jesus and to trust the narrator to know that the chief priests stirred up the crowd to pressure Pilate to crucify Jesus.

Analysis of these logical syllogisms in Mark 15:1–15 reveals that the chief priests and Pilate were the major actors behind the crucifixion of Jesus. The argumentative texture makes it clear that Barabbas is a strictly secondary figure, for he plays no role in the argument (the syllogism) itself. The discourse does not mention Barabbas earlier, and it never mentions him again. The crowd functions simply as the means by which the chief priests can enact their wish for Jesus; it has no positive intention for Barabbas.

There is also another dimension to the discourse: it characterizes the chief priests as people who act maliciously out of envy, and it characterizes Pilate as a person who tries to act benevolently but is vulnerable when the chief priests and the people in Jerusalem join together to make him act against his judgment. In rhetorical terms, this discourse combines epideictic and judicial rhetoric. Epideictic rhetoric evokes the context of a civil ceremony (like a funeral oration) by using praise and censure (blame) to persuade people to hold or reaffirm values in the present. Judicial rhetoric, in contrast, evokes the context of a courtroom by using accusation and acquittal to persuade an audience to make a judgment about events that occurred in the past (Kennedy 1984: 19). On the one hand, the discourse in Mark 15 is epideictic, praising Pilate and blaming the chief priests. On the other hand, it is judicial, pronouncing the chief priests guilty of staging the crucifixion of Jesus and acquitting Pilate of any premeditation, or even desire, to crucify Jesus. Pilate, so the narrative implies, delivered Jesus over for crucifixion only because he got "caught" in the context of a setting of his usual benevolence — releasing a prisoner to the people in Jerusalem each year at their Passover festival.

Markan discourse had already set the stage for the death of Jesus in 14:1b-2, characterizing the chief priests and scribes as seeking a special way to arrest and kill Jesus because "they were afraid" of a riot among the people if they killed him during the festival. Narrational discourse makes it clear that the chief priests and scribes want to kill Jesus. As the story progressed, narrational discourse gave a series of reasons why they may want to kill him:

a. Jesus had refused to respond clearly to chief priests, scribes, and elders in public concerning the authority by which he was doing the things he did (11:27–33).

b. Jesus told a parable against them. The parable featured keepers of a vineyard who beat and killed people the owner sent to them to get a share of the produce from the vineyard (12:1–12).

c. Jesus made fun in public of the position of the scribes that the Messiah is the son of David. The crowd gained pleasure at the expense of the public honor of the scribes when Jesus did this (12:35–37).

d. Jesus described the scribes as wealthy people who seek public honor and devour widows' houses (12:38–40).

e. Some people claimed that Jesus said he would destroy the temple and build another (14:58).

f. Jesus said under questioning that he was the Messiah, the Son of the Blessed (14:62).

In the midst of these specific situations, Markan discourse suggests that the chief priests and scribes feared the popularity of Jesus (14:2).

After the narrative presents these events and concerns, narrational comment in the scene featuring Jesus and Pilate together "reads the mind of Pilate" twice:

a. For he perceived that it was out of envy that the chief priests had delivered him up. (15:10)

b. So Pilate, wishing to satisfy the crowd, released for them Barabbas; and having scourged Jesus, he delivered him to be crucified. (15:15)

This all-knowing narrational commentary differentiates the chief priests from Pilate in the events of the crucifixion. Pilate plays the role of asking questions and drawing conclusions on the basis of the answers he does or does not get. The narrational discourse knows what is in the mind of Pilate concerning the chief priests and the crowd, but it does not suggest what Pilate is thinking about concerning himself. Pilate's thinking, then, functions as part of the argumentative texture of the text. The characterization of the chief priests as "envious" and the crowd as "impetuous" contribute to the syllogistic reasoning in the discourse.

When narrational commentary adds two more pieces of information, the interpretation of the scene is complete:

a. Now at the feast he (Pilate) used to release for them one prisoner for whom they asked. (15:6)

b. But the chief priests stirred up the crowd to have him release for them Barabbas instead. (15:11)

Pilate, according to the narrational commentary, got caught in a "necessity" to crucify Jesus for two reasons. The primary reason was that he regularly performed a benevolent act for the people in Jerusalem in honor of their Passover festival. The attendant reason was that the chief priests, who represent the families who have political power in the temple, staged the event as a result of their envy of Jesus. According to the narrational interpretation of the scene, then, chief priests used Pilate's benevolence as an opportunity to force Pilate to crucify Jesus.

The second scene (15:16–24) presents a logical progression: the soldiers crucify Jesus because Pilate, at the behest of the crowd, agreed to do so and handed Jesus over to the soldiers to perform the task. But this scene embeds a qualitative progression in its context. The implied reader/hearer expects that the soldiers will abuse Jesus, but there is no logical requirement that they put royal clothes on him and mock him as a pseudo-king. Yet the action flows naturally from the preceding episode, where Pilate repetitively referred to Jesus as "the King of the Jews." This is the nature of a qualitative progression: the implied reader/hearer had no reason to know that mockery in this form would occur (even if one has remembered Mark 8:31–10:34), but when it does occur it seems a natural outcome of previous events. The result is the amplification of a logical progression (crucifixion) with a qualitative progression (mockery as a pseudo-king).

The one instance of attributed speech in the second scene introduces the reasons and the nature of the actions in the scene — the soldiers are mocking Jesus as a "king" on the basis of the identification of Jesus as "the King of the Jews" in the preceding episode.

The third scene (15:25–32) is a qualitative progression. Once Jesus has been mocked, abused, and hung on the cross, the only logical necessity is death, whether it be quickly or slowly. This scene, instead, features additional mockery. As it unfolds, the action appears completely natural, but it is not necessary that passersby, chief priests and scribes, and those crucified with Jesus speak out in mockery and derision. In fact, one might expect that someone standing nearby, or one of the men being crucified alongside Jesus, might speak a kind word to Jesus. Lukan discourse, as we know, does feature one of the crucified men in such a role (Luke 23:39–43). The Markan scene unfolds programmatic action of mockery and spite, and the reader/hearer accepts it as a natural, though not necessary, outcome of previous events.

The fourth scene (Mark 15:33–39) features a logical progression: the purpose for crucifying Jesus was to kill him, and in this scene he dies. Narrational discourse, however, embellishes the scene with a number of qualitative features: (a) darkness for three hours, at the end of which Jesus dies; (b) a death cry in a foreign language that the discourse translates for implied hearers/readers, but which some actors in the scene misunderstand; (c) running to get a sponge of vinegar while he hangs on the cross; (d) splitting of the curtain of the temple in two, from top to bottom; and (e) a statement from a centurion that Jesus is son of God. Implied hearers/readers expect, or at least hope, that some kind of special signs or activities will occur at the death of this special person. The particular manifestations, however, regularly occur in qualitative progressions. The reader does not know exactly what to expect, but the reader accepts whatever unusual things happen. In this instance, the universe becomes dark for three hours, and the curtain of the temple splits in two from top to bottom. We will discuss the possible meanings of these events in upcoming sections. At this point we simply observe that they are qualitative progressions that help to define for the reader/hearer the nature of Jesus and the significance of his death.

The fifth scene (15:40–41) presents a qualitative progression. The reader had no reason to suspect that three women had been accompanying Jesus and the Twelve as they traveled from Galilee to Jerusalem. Once the reader is told, their presence seems fully acceptable, especially since one of the functions they performed on the way (serving Jesus) was the same as Peter's mother-in-law performed after Jesus had taken her by the hand and her fever had left her (1:31).

There may be debate whether the sixth scene (15:42–46) presents a logical or a qualitative progression. One of the conventional expectations may be that the body of the person would remain on the cross until birds would pick away at it. Then the bones would simply be thrown on a heap with other bones. To the extent that these expectations are not met, therefore, it can be argued that this scene contains a qualitative progression. However, the multiple rationales suggest that this passage can also be understood as a logical progression. These rationales include: (*a*) evening had come (15:42); (*b*) it was the day of preparation — the day before the sabbath (15:42); (*c*) Joseph of Arimathea was a respected member of the council (15:43); and (*d*) Joseph was looking for the kingdom of God. The narrational discourse has covered a lot of bases. Overall, the narration presents the following syllogistic reasoning:

[**Unstated major premise:** Respected representatives of the people of Israel remove the body of a dead person from a cross and place it in a tomb before night approaches, at least if the coming day is a sabbath.]

Minor premise: Jesus died in midafternoon.

Conclusion: Therefore, Joseph of Arimathea, a respected member of the council, requested permission to remove Jesus' body from the cross.

We will analyze this syllogism in the section on intertexture, since one of the issues is whether Joseph was fulfilling a specific directive in the Torah when he requested the body of Jesus and laid it in a tomb while there was still daylight.

The seventh scene (15:47–16:8) presents a final qualitative progression supported by the logic of social custom and the characterization of the women in the narrative. Since Joseph had bought a linen cloth, wrapped Jesus' corpse with this cloth, and laid it in a tomb, Jesus' body was prepared for burial and placed where it would remain until it decomposed. Social custom, however, suggests that women should complete a burial by putting aromatic ointments on the body. Also, the portrayal of the women as people who serve the needs of Jesus make it natural for them to attend to his body even at death. While the logic of the narrative does not require the women to anoint Jesus' body in the tomb, both social logic and the implicit logic of the characterization of the women make an unexpected activity seem fully natural for the reader. This is the nature of a qualitative progression at its best.

The argumentative texture of the Markan account of the crucifixion, then, features logical progression from the chief priests' maneuvering of the execution of Jesus by crucifixion through the crucifixion and death of Jesus. In the context of this logical progression, qualitative progressions amplify the account as the soldiers mock Jesus as a pseudo-king, as passersby and the two criminals on crosses beside Jesus taunt and revile him, as special phenomena accompany Jesus' death, as a respected member of the council arranges for and carries out the burial of Jesus' body, and as women go to the tomb because they want to anoint Jesus' body for a proper burial.

Narrational discourse, then, takes the form of argumentative discourse as it provides reasons for the events throughout the episode. Jesus was crucified *because* chief priests and scribes of the Jerusalem temple were envious of him. Pilate simply was trapped by a custom he usually performed at Passover, and the particular selection of Jesus as the one who was mocked and hung up was the result of the temple leaders' manipulation of the crowd who had gathered for the festival. The soldiers mocked and abused Jesus *because* Pilate had established an ironic definition of him as "the King of the Jews." People who passed by while Jesus hung on the cross with an inscription "the King of the Jews" over it mocked him *because* he said he would destroy the temple. Chief priests with scribes joined in the mockery, saying that *because* he is the Messiah, the King of Israel, he should save himself and come down from the cross. In the next scene, people mock Jesus *because* he cries out "Eloi," but the centurion calls him "son of God" *because* of what he has seen and heard. Joseph of Arimathea, *because* he was a respectable man expecting the kingdom of God, and *because* it was the day before the sabbath, requested the body for burial. *Because* Pilate was amazed that Jesus was already dead, the centurion functions as a witness to Pilate (and the reader) to Jesus' actual death in so short a period of time. *Because* three women responded to Jesus already in Galilee in such a manner that they have followed him to Jerusalem and served his needs during this time, they observe the events, including where Joseph puts Jesus' body. *Because* the women remain faithful to their role of serving Jesus, they find an empty tomb and receive news that Jesus is not there but has gone before the disciples to Galilee.

Argumentative texture, then, gives reasons for events to happen as they do. In some instances, the reasons are so explicit that a reader perceives them to be logical. In other instances, the reasons are implicit, part of the innate qualities of people, circumstances, and images that persuade people to accept their plausibility. In the context of both logically explicit and qualitatively innate reasons, unexpected things may happen in the story that the reader develops a willingness to accept as a natural outcome of the assertions and activities in the discourse.

F. Sensory-Aesthetic Texture and Pattern

The sensory-aesthetic texture of a text resides prominently in the range of senses the text evokes or embodies (thought, emotion, sight, sound, touch, smell) and the manner in which the text evokes or embodies them (reason, intuition, imagination, humor, etc.). An interpreter's identification of different "types" of literature (overall texts) and different "forms" in literature (shorter forms like proverb, riddle, or parable) is an initial insight into different sensory-aesthetic textures. Thus, a letter has a different sensory-aesthetic texture than a historical account, and a philosophical essay has a different sensory-aesthetic texture than a letter. But different letters and different historical accounts also may have different sensory-aesthetic textures: they may appeal to emotions or values in different ways; use a much more "personal" or "formal" approach; contain highly different shorter "forms"; and so on. Attentiveness to sensory-aesthetic texture may reveal dimensions that provide tone and perhaps even color to the discourse. In some instances, the discourse may be so rich and vivid that it evokes images as full and dramatic as cinema. In other instances, the discourse may work with images that evoke feelings of cold, hard fact or abstract logic. Thus, sensory-aesthetic texture may call attention to dimensions that give particular tone and color to repetitive, progressive, narrational, or argumentative texture in the discourse.

One way to search for sensory-aesthetic texture and pattern can be to identify and group every aspect of a text that refers to a part of the body (like eyes, ears, nose, etc.) and to actions or perceptions related to a part of the body (like seeing, hearing, smelling, etc.). In the section above on progressive texture, there already was some discussion of seeing in the Markan account of the crucifixion, burial, and resurrection of Jesus.

Another way is to identify "body zones" in the discourse. Bruce Malina has concluded that descriptions of human behavior in the New Testament depict persons and events concretely. Interaction is described metaphorically, for the most part, using parts of the human person as metaphors. A human being is endowed with a heart for thinking, along with eyes that fill the heart with data; a mouth for speaking, along with ears that collect the speech of others; and hands and feet for acting. Thus, humans consist of three mutually interpenetrating yet distinguishable zones of interacting with their environments: the zone of emotion-fused thought, the zone of self-expressive speech, and the zone of purposeful action. Using this approach creates a taxonomy of three body zones and their related phenomena in the thought-world of Mediterranean culture:

> a. *Zone of emotion-fused thought:* eyes, heart, eyelids, pupils, and the activities of these organs — to see, know, understand, think, remember, choose, feel, consider, look at. The following representative nouns and adjectives pertain to this zone as well: thought, intelligence, mind, wisdom, folly, intention, plan, will, affection, love, hate, sight, regard, blindness, look; intelligent, loving, wise, foolish, hateful, joyous, sad, and the like.

In our culture, this zone would cover the areas we refer to as in-
tellect, will, judgment, conscience, personality thrust, core personality,
affection, and so forth.

b. *Zone of self-expressive speech:* mouth, ears, tongue, lips, throat, teeth,
jaws, and the activities of these organs — to speak, hear, say, call, cry,
question, sing, recount, tell, instruct, praise, listen to, blame, curse,
swear, disobey, turn a deaf ear to. The following nouns and adjectives pertain to this zone as well: speech, voice, call, cry, clamor, song,
sound, hearing; eloquent, dumb, talkative, silent, attentive, distracted,
and the like.

In our culture, this zone would cover the area we refer to as self-
revelation through speech, communication with others, the human as
listener who dialogues with others in a form of mutual self-unveiling,
and so on.

c. *Zone of purposeful action:* hands, feet, arms, fingers, legs, and the activities of these organs — to do, act, accomplish, execute, intervene,
touch, come, go, march, walk, stand, sit, along with specific activities
such as to steal, kidnap, commit adultery, build, and the like. The following representative nouns and adjectives pertain to this zone: action,
gesture, work, activity, behavior, step, walking, way, course, and any
specific activity; active, capable, quick, slow, and so forth.

In our culture, this zone would cover the area of outward human
behavior, all external activity, human actions upon the world of persons
and things. (Malina 1993: 73–77)

Mark 15:1–16:8 begins with Jesus' body, with its hands bound, being
handed forcefully over to Pilate (15:1). The following verses then emphasize
the use of mouths and ears. Pilate speaks to Jesus; Jesus hears and responds
(15:2). Then the chief priests accuse Jesus many times. When Pilate invites
Jesus to respond to the accusations of the chief priests, Jesus does not speak,
and he does not use his mouth for speech again until he cries out at his death
(15:34). In a context where Jesus is not able to use his hands for purposeful
action, and the movement of his feet is dictated by people who lead him here
and there, Jesus no longer uses his mouth. This is a dramatic development in
the story of Jesus, a person who was described openly as a teacher the first
time he entered a synagogue (1:21–28) and a person who is repeatedly characterized as a teacher throughout the narrative (Robbins 1992a). A central
feature of the characterization of Jesus now abruptly ceases to function in the
narrative. One could imagine that Jesus would have taught both Pilate and
the chief priests about the kingdom of God and about true kingship. This is,
in fact, what Jesus does in the Gospel of John (18:28–38). But not in the
Gospel of Mark. The identity of Jesus emerges at the end of the Gospel of

Mark not through Jesus' speech as a teacher but through things that happen to his body.

When Jesus does not respond to the accusations against him, a new aspect of Pilate's body comes into view. The narrator now refers to Pilate's emotion-fused thought. Pilate marvels that Jesus does not use his mouth against the many accusations made against him (15:5). The narrator uses this same mode of emotion-fused thought earlier in the story to describe people's reaction in the Decapolis to the Gerasene demoniac's account of what Jesus had done for him (5:20). Also, the narrator uses this emotion to describe Jesus' reaction in Nazareth to people's disbelief (6:6). Now this emotion describes Pilate's disbelief that Jesus does not speak out and refute the accusations against him. Amazement in Pilate's mind, then, momentarily replaces Pilate's use of his mouth for speech as the narrator recounts that it was customary to release a prisoner during the Passover feast. Immediately again, however, mouths and ears dominate the scene as Pilate converses with the crowd about Jesus' body. In the end, Pilate frees the body of Barabbas and hands the body of Jesus over to be whipped and crucified.

Soldiers play a game with Jesus' body in the second scene (15:16–24). They dress it up and undress it like naughty, violent children playing with a doll. They focus their attack on the head of Jesus — the body zone of his thought, feeling, seeing, hearing, and speech. There is no special attack on his ears or eyes. They do not, for instance, cut off an ear or gouge out an eye. These remain whole and in place to the end. Rather, his head as the center of his mode of understanding, feeling, and intention attracts the most attention. They put a crown of thorns on Jesus' head, they salute it, and they hit his head with a stick. Then, however, they mock Jesus' mouth, using their own mouths to spit on him and wag their jaws at his unspeaking lips, jaws, and tongue. Then they play with his entire body, dressing it up in purple, then un-dressing it. Only after they have played violently and flippantly with his body do the soldiers lead this "body" out to crucify it. Through all of this, Jesus has said nothing, and narrational discourse does not speak for Jesus' mind. It is as though Jesus has become not only speechless but also mindless. Earlier in the narrative, Jesus often reads the minds of others and speaks to them directly, powerfully, and authoritatively. Now the narrator speaks neither of thought nor of speech in relation to Jesus' body. The actively thinking, perceiving, willing, and exhorting Jesus has become a passively mute body that people lead around, beat, mock, spit on, and play with as they wish. There is a mo-ment, however, when this passivity is broken. When they offer Jesus drugged wine, he does not let them put it in his mouth (15:23). Words no longer come out of his mouth. He also does not allow drink to go into it to relieve his pain. His mouth has become closed, both for giving and for receiving.

The next scene (15:25–32) introduces time into the mode of perception in the discourse. It was early in the morning, the beginning of daylight, when the chief priests, elders, scribes, and the whole sanhedrin handed Jesus over to Pilate. The activities that followed filled three hours. Now Jesus' body begins to hang on the cross. At this point, mockery of Jesus' body is not limited to the soldiers. Everything in the scene mocks his body. The cross itself mocks Jesus' body with an inscription that calls him "the King of the Jews." People who pass by mock his body with their mouths and their heads, taunting him to bring his body to action by coming down from the cross. Chief priests and scribes also mock his body with their mouths, reconfiguring the inscription on the cross to ridicule him as "the Messiah, the King of Israel." But then they add a reference to eyes and heart. "Come down," they say, "that we may see and believe." Just as Pilate's encounter with Jesus finally brought a response from inside his body — namely, he marveled that Jesus no longer spoke — now the chief priests and scribes evoke an awareness of eyes that see and hearts that believe. In turn, those who are crucified with Jesus utter words of reproach against him. In this scene, then, the relation of Jesus to the people around him is reversed. Earlier in the narrative, Jesus powerfully used his eyes, head, and mouth to challenge people to see and believe. In this scene, people energetically use their mouths and heads to mock what they see and to ridicule what Jesus has asked people to believe.

The next scene (15:33–39) begins with another reference to time. It took three hours for the door to close on any hope for Jesus' release. During this time, Jesus' speech stopped, his body was beaten and mocked, and his body was led off to be hung on a cross. Now the narration tells us that Jesus' body hung on the cross as an object of ridicule and shame for as long as it had taken for the public pretense of a trial, the physical abuse and mockery by the soldiers, and the journey to Golgotha at the beginning of the day. At the end of this time period, according to the narrator, the universe itself responded. The response was not a flash of light, a roar of thunder, a miraculous release of the body from the cross, and a glorious ascent of the body into heaven. Rather, the light that the earth gives forth during the day to give life to the world suddenly became darkness. In other words, the universe itself became passive, much as Jesus' body became passive during the scene with Pilate. Not only did all people forsake him, but the universe itself — with God as its inward center of emotion, thought, and will — withdrew into passivity. And the universe remained in this passive state for three hours, the same length of time as the opening series of events and the same length of time during which Jesus' body hung on the cross in ridicule and shame.

After three hours of passivity in the universe, Jesus cries out with a loud voice, "Eloi, Eloi, lema sabachthani," which the narrator immediately translates as "My God, my God, why have you forsaken me?" (15:34). But this simply brings forth more mockery. Some people standing by think Jesus has called out to Elijah. One of them runs, fills a sponge with vinegar, and extends it to Jesus on a stick so he will drink it and revive himself long enough to see if Elijah will come and help him. Instead, Jesus gives out his death gasp (15:37). At this point, the universe responds by splitting the curtain of the temple in two from top to bottom (15:38). In turn, when the centurion who is standing opposite the cross sees Jesus give out his last breath, he speaks out saying, "Truly this man is son of God." Finally, in other words, both the universe and someone near Jesus respond in a manner other than ridicule and mockery. But not until the moment of Jesus' death. Only when every function in Jesus' body has shut down, including the hope in Jesus' mind that perhaps it will be God's will to "take this cup from him" (14:36), is there some kind of response that affirms the meaning of Jesus' life. But what do these responses mean? What meanings do the splitting of the temple curtain evoke? What meanings attend the title son of God when it occurs on the lips of a Roman centurion? We must pursue these meanings in later sections.

In any case, in this scene Jesus once again uses his mouth. But Jesus uses his mouth not to teach but to cry out in despair after three hours of passivity in the universe in addition to the earlier hours of passivity in his body. One might have hoped that when Jesus became passive, the universe would have gone into action. Instead, the universe itself symbiotically moved into passivity along with Jesus. Jesus, however, momentarily goes into action at death. At this point, the universe strikes out by splitting the curtain of the temple in two. In addition, a foreigner in the land of Israel "sees" how Jesus dies and "speaks out." What does the future hold?

The narration does not stop here. Ironically and casually, it seems at first, narrational discourse indicates that three women observed all of these events from a distance. Recalling the zone of purposeful action, however, we can observe more fully the nature of the narrative description of the women. These women were followers of Jesus from the time he was in Galilee through the time when he came into Jerusalem. They did not flee when the other followers did; they simply remained at a distance to observe everything they could. These women "served" Jesus during the time he was traveling from Galilee to Jerusalem. Therefore, they have been engaged in purposeful activity for a significant period of time. Moreover, this is the activity angels performed when Jesus was in the wilderness prior to his entrance into Galilee (1:13). It is good activity. Peter's mother-in-law also performed this kind of activity after Jesus removed her fever (1:31). And this was the activity Jesus said that the Son of man came to perform and that those who wish to be first and great must perform (10:43–45). This narration, which appears to be simply a casual epilogue to the death of Jesus, recycles major topics of purposeful activity that occupy the narrative until the time Jesus is handed over to Pilate. Suddenly the topics of Galilee, following, serving, and going up to Jerusalem are on the table again, so to speak. Much as the universe and the centurion respond to the death of Jesus, so the narration has found a way to revive the meaning of Jesus' life in the context of the death of his body. For Markan narration, we recall, endings simply are new beginnings.

The narration continues by referring to time (15:42). Reference to time played a significant role in moving the narrative forward from the point when it announced the approach of Passover in 14:1. And, as we have seen, the narration uses time dramatically to move the story forward from the time Jesus was handed over to Pilate to the moment of Jesus' death. Now the narration moves decisively beyond Jesus' death by referring to time. The narration refers to three items of time: (a) evening; (b) preparation; and (c) the day before the sabbath. Evening, according to Jewish time during the first century, represents the end of one day and the beginning of another. Preparation regularly refers to the day prior to a festival, but it can also mean the day of preparing for the sabbath. The reference to time as preparation deepens the mode of purposeful action the discourse introduced with its initial characterization of the women (15:40–41). Joseph now embodies the kind of purposeful action attributed to the women as he requests the body of Jesus, takes it down from the cross, wraps it in linen cloth, and places it in a proper burial place.

Mark 15:42–46 focuses, naturally, on the entire body of Jesus. Joseph shows courage by activating his feet to go to Pilate and activating his mouth to request Jesus' body. Pilate once again responds with amazement (15:44). While earlier Pilate's amazement resulted in offering the crowd a choice to have Jesus or Barabbas released to them, here his amazement leads him to summon the centurion to verify that Jesus in fact has died this quickly. At this point, Jesus' corpse is the focus of attention in the narration. The centurion verifies that Jesus' body now is indeed only a corpse. Therefore, Pilate grants permission, and Joseph buys linen cloth, takes the corpse down, wraps it up, lays it in a tomb, and rolls a rock over the opening in the tomb.

Again the narration continues with a conclusion that is a new beginning. Mary Magdalene and Mary the mother of Joses observe where Joseph lays the corpse of Jesus. And again the narration introduces time. When the sabbath is over, all three women who had observed the crucifixion buy ointments to anoint Jesus' body. When the women find an open tomb with a young man dressed in a white robe sitting in it, the narration turns to emotion and emotion directs the activities of the women's bodies. The women are amazed at what they find, they run out of the tomb and flee when they hear the words of the young man, they tremble and their minds go into disarray, they are filled with fear, and they tell no one anything. Much as Jesus himself had come to a point of speechlessness, so the women no longer speak. They remain people of action, in accordance with the characterization of them in the previous narration. Earlier, they followed Jesus and served him. Seeing the crucifixion and the burial, they bought spices and came to the tomb to anoint Jesus' body. They are still filled with action. Filled with amazement, trembling, confusion, and fear, they flee from the tomb. But this is a move away from following rather than toward it. This was the response of the disciples earlier when Jesus was arrested (14:50). Now the women not only flee but also do not use their mouths to spread the information of what they have seen.

According to the earliest manuscripts, this is where the text of Mark ends.

One can see that the sensory-aesthetic texture of the ending moves rhythmically from action and speech inwardly to emotion and to action directed by emotion. Some interpreters think the narration had to continue further than 16:8. The sensory-aesthetic texture of the text, however, makes it clear that every ending is another beginning. Even the flight of the women, therefore, is not an ending that can remain an ending. Somehow, somewhere these women will enact the message of Jesus' death and resurrection in a form that transmits its meanings to other people's lives. The sensory-aesthetic mode in which this occurs moves beyond the mode of speech and action in teaching or the mode of speech and action in ruling others. Rather, the mode enacts a form of speech and action that embodies both the activity and the passivity of Jesus during this final time in the story. Jesus' feet had taken him toward Jerusalem. Jesus' mouth, hands, and feet had taken followers and others on a journey through healing, controversy, a vision of the future, service to others, and interpretation of the present. Now the task is left to those, both men and women, who find a way to embody this interactive mode of activity and passivity in daily life.

In summary, then, the sensory-aesthetic texture of the Gospel of Mark enacts a mode of action and speech that challenges alternative sensory-aesthetic modes of action and speech in the world. The sensory-aesthetic texture of the story itself challenges the innermost recesses of one's emotions, one's conceptual configurations, and one's will. Action is not enough. Passivity is not enough. Speech is not enough. Emotion is not enough. Will is not enough. Only a complexly interwoven matrix of activity, passivity, speech, emotion, and will mimetically enacts the sensory-aesthetic texture of the text.

Conclusion

Inner texture, then, leads the interpreter to explore repetitive, progressive, narrational, opening-middle-closing, argumentative, and sensory-aesthetic texture. This texture lies clearly in the words in the text itself. Simply pointing to inner texture should reveal it. The configuration of certain phenomena may be complex, but interpreters can negotiate this complexity, and disagree over it, by looking no further than the text itself.

It may be tempting, since all the data lie in the text itself, for interpreters to apply only this angle of approach to texts. Ironically, this angle did not attract central attention in scholarship during the nineteenth century and most of the twentieth century. Now that attention has swung to the inner texture of the text, however, some interpreters want to do nothing else. But here the last two centuries of scholarship sound out a clear warning. A text is always interacting somehow with phenomena outside itself. Therefore, we must turn to another aspect of the texture of texts. After a short guide that encourages the reader to explore the inner texture of the Markan account of Jesus' encounter with a rich man, the next chapter explores the nature of intertexture in texts.

STUDY GUIDE:
The Rich Man and Jesus in Mark 10:17–22

This is a study guide for exploring the "inner" texture of the story of the rich man and Jesus in Mark 10:17–22. Becoming familiar with the inner features of a text is a first step in achieving a "close reading" that reveals aspects of the text and its meanings that otherwise are easily overlooked.

The inner texture of a text creates the context for the inner meanings of the text. The most obvious characteristic of inner texture is its patterns of repetition and progression. These patterns point to the convictions expressed in the words in the text and to the manner in which the text attempts to persuade and convince the reader.

If a word or phrase is repeated twice in a unit of text, the first occurrence is the beginning of the theme and the second occurrence is its end. If a word or phrase is repeated three times, there is a beginning, middle, and end to the theme. If the word or phrase is repeated five or six times, the repetitions are likely to cluster together in a pattern that begins, continues, and ends the theme. Repetition, then, creates progression — either it creates a progression simply from a beginning to an end; or it creates a progression from a beginning, through a continuation, to an end.

Repetition and progression of words and phrases have only limited significance, unless an interpreter sees their place in the introduction, the body, and the conclusion of a complete rhetorical unit, like the story of the rich man and Jesus. An initial challenge is to discover where the introduction ends and the body begins, and where the conclusion begins and ends. This means, then, that the body of the unit also has a beginning and end, and it is informative to discover where that beginning and end is.

Regularly, repetition of words and phrases helps the interpreter determine the beginning and end of the introduction, body, and conclusion of the unit of text under consideration. Two occurrences of the same word may signal the beginning of the introduction, a different word repeated two or three times may signal the middle of the introduction, and then one or two more occurrences of the first word may signal the end of the introduction.

Different kinds of repetition in a text form different repetition patterns. Displaying this pattern on a written page often reveals interesting things about the unit of text that otherwise escape the interpreter. The questions and comments listed below are designed to help an interpreter uncover the inner texture of a unit of biblical text.

Another characteristic of inner texture is alternation between narration (the writer's or narrator's voice) and speech (the voice that the narration attributes to specific people). Sometimes an introduction consists entirely of the narrator's voice, and sometimes speech attributed to other people will appear already in the introduction. Various patterns also may appear in the body and the conclusion. The pattern of alternation between narration and attributed speech reveals an important aspect of the inner texture of the unit.

There are two dimensions to the inner texture of a unit: (*a*) the inner texture of the unit of text itself; and (*b*) the participation of this unit of text in the overall written document in which it occurs. This study guide begins with the unit of text first; then it moves to the participation of the unit in the overall text of the Gospel of Mark.

•

1. Read the story of the rich man and Jesus in Mark 10:17–22. It seems clear, does it not, that this unit has a clear beginning and a clear end? What is the basic action that opens the unit? What is the basic action that closes the unit?

2. Where does the introduction to the story end and the body of the story begin? Where does the conclusion to the story begin? Describe the nature of the introduction and the conclusion on the basis of the presence of narration and attributed speech in them.

3. Looking closely at the alternation between narration and attributed speech in the body of story, describe the "narration/attributed-speech" pattern. Identify the beginning, middle, and end of the body of the story. Is the middle part of the body the longest or the shortest section, or is the middle part of the body medium length in comparison to the beginning and end of the body of the story? Who speaks in the middle of the body of the story? Who speaks first and last in the attributed speech in the body of the story? In other words, who speaks the first and last word?

4. On a sheet of paper list the words that are repeated in the entire story. Now identify if the repeated words are located in the introduction, the body, or the conclusion of the story. What patterns of repetition do you see?

5. Does the conclusion repeat anything that occurs in the introduction? Why is there or is there not any repetition? Does the conclusion show a continuation of the themes in the introduction, or has something opposite occurred that stops the continuation of the themes?

6. In the body of the story, identify the initial unit, the middle unit, and the final unit. Now identify the repetition throughout the three units in the body of the story.

a. What word that was in the introduction is repeated at the beginning of the initial unit in the body of the story? Would it be fair to say that the repetition of this word at the beginning of the body of the story creates a beginning for the initial unit in the body of the story? What sequence of words is repeated five times in the remainder of the initial unit in the body of the story? How is the final statement in this initial unit different from the five statements that precede it? Does it seem correct to speak of a beginning, middle, and ending for the initial unit in the body of the story?

b. One word in the middle unit repeats a word used earlier in the story. What is the word, and to whom is the word attributed?

c. Describe the final unit in relation to the initial and middle unit. Describe the nature of the progression from the initial and middle unit to the final unit in the body of the story. Do you see a common mood of speech (in the technical sense of indicative, imperative, and subjunctive mood) in the initial and final unit of the body of the story? What is the name of this mood, and what is its function?

7. At this point, it will be informative to correlate aspects of the inner texture of our unit about the rich man and Jesus with aspects of the inner texture of the overall Gospel of Mark. What title does the rich man use twice for Jesus in this story? This is a favorite title people use in the Gospel of Mark when they address Jesus. Write down the different individual people and groups that address Jesus with this title in Mark 4:38; 5:35; 9:17, 38; 10:35, 51; 12:14, 19, 32; 13:1; 14:14. Also make a list of the narrator's use of the verb and noun associated with this title in Mark 1:21, 22, 27; 2:13; 4:1, 2; 6:2, 6, 30, 34; 7:7; 8:31; 9:31; 10:1; 11:17, 18; 12:14, 35, 38; 14:49. Who is the subject of the verb in the narrator's sentences? What, then, was one of the major activities of Jesus, according to the Gospel of Mark, and what title was used to refer to this activity?

8. What is the final command Jesus makes to the rich man in the body of the story (10:21)? Compare this with Mark 1:18; 2:14, 15; 3:7; 5:24; 6:1; 8:34; 9:38; 10:28, 32, 52; 15:41. What is unusual about the response of the man to Jesus' command in this story, in contrast to the other occurrences of the command?

9. In the tradition of form criticism, interpreters use terms like "parable," "miracle story," "story about Jesus" (where something happens to Jesus, like the baptism), and "pronouncement story" to describe units in the Gospels (see Bailey and Vander Broek 1992: 91–156). What terms would you use to describe the form of this story?

Chapter 2

Intertexture

ENTERING THE INTERACTIVE WORLD
OF A TEXT

Intertexture is a text's representation of, reference to, and use of phenomena in the "world" outside the text being interpreted. In other words, the intertexture of a text is the interaction of the language in the text with "outside" material and physical "objects," historical events, texts, customs, values, roles, institutions, and systems.

The text "configures" phenomena outside the text in a particular language environment. This environment of language claims, implicitly or explicitly, either to "represent" external phenomena accurately or to be an adventure, implicitly or explicitly, in "creating" phenomena that relate in some provocative way to phenomena outside the text. A major goal of intertextual analysis is to ascertain the nature and result of processes of configuration and reconfiguration of phenomena in the world outside the text. Sometimes the text imitates another text but places different people in it. Sometimes it restructures a well-known tradition so that it ends differently or has very different implications for belief and action. Sometimes it inverts a tradition, turning the rhetoric of a previous situation on its head to create a new and distinct dramatic tradition. In each instance, the result is a text with a rich configuration of texts, cultures, and social and historical phenomena.

A. Oral-Scribal Intertexture

One of the ways a text configures and reconfigures is to use, either explicitly or without reference, language from other texts. There are five basic ways in which language in a text uses language that exists in another text: recitation, recontextualization, reconfiguration, narrative amplification, and thematic elaboration. Oral-scribal intertexture involves a text's use of any other text outside of itself, whether it is an inscription, the work of a Greek poet, noncanonical apocalyptic material, or the Hebrew Bible.

I. Recitation

Recitation is the transmission of speech or narrative, from either oral or written tradition, in the exact words in which the person has received the speech or narrative or in different words.

    a. Replication of exact words of another written text. Recitation may present a "photocopy," an exact duplicate of words in another written text. An example is Mark 7:10a: "For Moses said, 'Honor your father and your mother.'" The quotation itself (not "For Moses said") presents the exact string of eight Greek words that stand in common between Exod 20:1 and Deut 5:16 (Dean-Otting and Robbins 1993: 111). This is an exact, verbatim word-string that people easily and regularly committed to memory in antiquity. Attributing the quotation to Moses ("For Moses said") signals the awareness of a written text that was probably read regularly to people in the synagogue. When the text includes "For Moses said," it creates a chreia (pronounced "kray-a"). A chreia is a brief statement or action aptly attributed to a specific person or something analogous to a person (Mack and Robbins 1989: 11). A chreia may have the form of a "sayings chreia," an "action chreia," or a "mixed chreia" that attributes both speech and action to a particular person (Hock and O'Neil 1986: 85–89). Creating a chreia using words from a previously written text is a common characteristic of rhetorical culture. The New Testament contains many chreiai (the plural of "chreia," pronounced "kray-eye") attributed to Jesus, Peter, Paul, and others. As noticed in the previous chapter, narration may or may not attribute voice to specific characters in the narrative. Attributing speech to a particular person or text from the past evokes an explicit image of a person or text in the world outside the inner texture of the text. Attributing speech directly to a person creates a vividness and specificity that encourages the reader to accept the "reality" of this person in the world outside the text. For this reason, chreiai are innately intertextual — they evoke traditions, events, texts, and people in the world outside the inner texture of the text being interpreted.

    b. Replication of exact words with one or more differences. Recitation may present almost an exact copy, differing only one or more ways from another written text. An example is John 2:17: "His disciples remembered that it was written, 'Zeal for thy house will consume me.'" In Ps 69:9 the text reads, "Zeal for thy house *has* consumed me."

    c. Omission of words in such a manner that the word-string has the force of a proverb, maxim, or authoritative judgment. Recitation may leave certain words out to make the statement brief and crisp. An example is 1 Cor 1:31: "Therefore, as it is written, 'Let him who boasts, boast in the Lord.'" This verse is an abbreviation of:

> "But *in* this *let him who boasts boast,* understanding and knowing that I am *the Lord* who does mercy and justice and righteousness on the earth; for in these things are my will," says the Lord. (Jer 9:24)

When the text of 1 Corinthians omits the many words that it does, it creates a statement that functions like a forceful proverb or maxim: "Let him who boasts, boast in the Lord."

   d. *Recitation of a saying using words different from the authoritative source.* The ancient rhetorician Theon of Alexandria recommends that writers learn how to recite not only "in the same words" but "in other words as well" (Hock and O'Neil 1986: 95). An excellent instance of this exists in Paul's recitation of the command of the Lord "that those who proclaim the gospel should get their living from the gospel" (1 Cor 9:14). This exists in other written texts in the following form:

> [Jesus said,] "For the laborer is worthy of his food [or: reward]." (Matt 10:10 [Luke 10:7])

This is an instance where a Pauline text recites a saying of Jesus in different words than the words with which other people recite it when they attribute it to Jesus. Paul claims to be reciting "a command of the Lord," but the words in the text are common words Paul, rather than Jesus, used. The verb "to proclaim" does not occur regularly in early Christian language outside of Paul's writings, and the noun "gospel" does not occur in the earliest layers of sayings attributed to Jesus (Kloppenborg 1988: 220; Mack 1993). Thus, 1 Cor 9:14 uses "Paul's words" in this "quotation" of the Lord Jesus. Pauline discourse does not so freely use different words when it is reciting written biblical text; rather, it freely "omits" and rearranges words but usually does not substitute entirely different words.

   e. *Recitation that uses some of the narrative words in the biblical text plus a saying from the text.* It is natural for New Testament texts to tell a story using a few of the same words the Old Testament text uses to identify the people in the story and to present basic action that leads up to a dramatic recitation of a saying attributed to a person. Acts 7:30–32 reads as follows:

> Now when forty years had passed, *an angel appeared to him* in the wilderness of Mount Sinai, *in the flame* of a *burning bush.* When *Moses* saw it, he was amazed at *the sight;* and as he approached to look, there came the voice of the *Lord:* "*I am the God of Abraham, Isaac, and Jacob.*" *Moses* began to tremble and did not dare to look.

The text that tells this story in Exod 3:2–6 is much longer than the text in Acts 7:30–32. The text in Acts uses its own words (influenced by words elsewhere in the Bible) to tell the story briefly, and it recites some exact words (italicized) that appear in Exod 3:2–6.

   Acts 7:30–32 presents "recitation both of narrative and of saying in an abbreviated form," a skill that Theon thought students should learn during the first century C.E. (Hock and O'Neil 1986: 100–101). In other words, the recitation abbreviates not only the narrative wording but also the wording of the saying. In Exod 3:6 the saying of the Lord reads:

> I myself *am the God* of your father, the God *of Abraham, and* the God
> of *Isaac, and* the God of *Jacob.*

The recitation of the saying in Acts omits many of the words, presenting only
the italicized words: "I am the God of Abraham and Isaac and Jacob." This
abbreviated recitation suggests the presence of the expanded written version
somewhere in the vicinity where the person wrote the version in Acts. The
abbreviated account does not vary "factually" from the written version. There
is no special concern to duplicate extended word-strings in exact form, but
neither is there any embarrassment about repeating words exactly. There is
freedom to use one's own words to recite the account in a manner that gives
the recitation an appropriate function in its context (Robbins 1991b). This
kind of recitation is frequent in Luke and Acts.

f. Recitation of a narrative in substantially one's own words. Mark 2:25–26
is an example:

> And he said to them, "Have you never read what *David* did when he
> and the ones *with* him were hungry and in need of food? He entered
> the house of God, when Abiathar was high priest, and ate *the bread of
> the Presence,* which it is not lawful for any but the *priests* to *eat,* and he
> gave some to his companions."

Words that occur in 1 Sam 21:1–6 are italicized. The remaining words are
different from the biblical text. A remarkable feature of this recitation is that
it does not get the story quite right (Mack and Robbins 1989: 114–17; Dean-
Otting and Robbins 1993: 97–103). It is an abbreviated recitation that reveals
no close relation to the written version. This type of recitation, common in
"rhetorical cultures," replicates only words that are easily transmitted in oral
transmission apart from any "authoritative" version of the text, and it contains a significant number of variations from the written text that a "literary
culture" would consider to be errors.

g. Recitation that summarizes a span of text that includes various episodes. The
full text of Luke 17:26–27 reads:

> Just as it was in the days of *Noah,* so it will be in the days of the Son of
> Man. They were eating and drinking, and marrying and being given in
> marriage, until the day Noah entered the ark, and the flood came and
> destroyed them all.

This recitation presents a summary of the text in Gen 6:1–24. There is no
reference to "eating and drinking" in the Old Testament account. This appears to be a result of the characterization of the Son of man's "eating and
drinking" (Matt 11:19; Luke 7:33). The reference to "marrying and being
given in marriage" summarizes Gen 6:2–4, which emphasizes the marrying
between "sons of God" and "daughters of men." In addition, the older text
features Noah and all of his household entering the ark (Gen 7:1, 7), while

the recitation focuses on Noah alone. There is no evidence of direct interaction between the wording in this saying attributed to Jesus and the wording in the account in Genesis. The wording of the saying is characteristic of oral expansion in a rhetorical culture, without concern for wording in the actual written text of the account.

It is remarkable that there are no instances of recitation of scripture in the Markan account of the crucifixion (see Marcus 1992: 153). There is, however, recitation of an inscription and of a "previous saying of Jesus" in Mark 15. Recitation of the inscription occurs in 15:26:

> And the inscription of the charge against him read, "The King of the Jews."

This verse establishes intertextual reference to written text outside the text of the Gospel of Mark. It is informative that scholars regularly have considered this inscription to be one of the most secure "historical facts" about the crucifixion. Markan discourse has been very successful indeed, but one of the reasons is the discourse in the other Gospels. Matthean discourse strengthens the reality and importance of the inscription by attributing it to action by the soldiers, in other words, by making it an action chreia:

> And over his head they put the charge against him, which read: "This is Jesus the King of the Jews." (Matt 27:37)

This Matthean account recites the inscription with two significant differences. First, the Markan recitation does not suggest that the name "Jesus" was on the inscription. Second, the Markan recitation does not suggest the presence of the phrase "this is." Thus, there are actually three differences between the Markan and Matthean recitation: (*a*) soldiers put on the cross the inscription of the charge against Jesus; (*b*) the inscription contains the name "Jesus" as well as the title "the King of the Jews"; and (*c*) the inscription also contains the phrase "this is." The exact words on the inscription, then, vary between the Markan and the Matthean account.

The Lukan account proceeds somewhat differently from both Mark and Matthew. When the narration *recites* the inscription, it does not call the inscription "the charge against Jesus"; it does not say that the soldiers put the inscription on the cross; and it does not include the name "Jesus" on the inscription. It does, however, say that the phrase "this is" was on the inscription. To understand how Lukan discourse presents the recitation of the inscription, we must observe another thing about "chreia composition" during the first century.

People who learned to write in Greek were taught through a process of writing and rewriting short sayings and anecdotes a teacher knew either from popular lore or from reading available literature. Theon of Alexandria, who wrote a treatise in Greek on the current state of these activities during the time period when the New Testament Gospels were being written (50–100 c.e.), lists the exercises a student would perform:

1. Recitation
2. Inflection (different cases, persons, and numbers)
3. Commentary
4. Critique
5. Expansion
6. Abbreviation
7. Refutation
8. Confirmation (see Mack and Robbins 1989: 36–41; Hock and O'Neil 1986: 94–107; Robbins 1993c: xii–xiv)

Lukan discourse presents the inscription on the cross as a "commentary" on a chreia (exercise 3). Here is how it presents it:

> [36]The soldiers also mocked him, coming up and offering him vinegar, [37]and saying, "If you are the King of the Jews, save yourself!" [38]There was also an inscription over him, "This is the King of the Jews." (Luke 23:36–38)

In contrast to the simple recitation of the inscription as "the charge against" Jesus in Mark and the recitation in Matthew of the inscription in the context of an action chreia that attributes the action to the soldiers, Luke 23:36–38 presents a sayings chreia that attributes mocking speech to the soldiers, and the recitation of the inscription occurs as a "commentary" on the chreia. In other words, Lukan discourse summarizes action and speech by the soldiers in an abbreviated chreia that recounts their "mockery," their "offering him vinegar," and their "taunting him as the King of the Jews to save himself." In this context, the reference to the inscription confirms and supplements the chreia. In Luke, there is no statement that the inscription recites "the charge against" Jesus. Rather, in the Lukan discourse the inscription is "additional comment" on "what has been fittingly and concisely said in the chreia" (Theon, cited in Hock and O'Neil 1986: 99). Thus, recitation of the inscription is a matter of recounting an additional "mockery of Jesus" while he was hanging on the cross. The effect of chreia narration by Lukan discourse is to characterize the inscription as an inaccurate legal charge against Jesus. According to the narration, the inscription is simply another part of the abusive mockery of Jesus on the cross.

Johannine discourse proceeds in a manner that differs still further from the Synoptic Gospels. The Gospel of John creates an expanded chreia (exercise 5 above) that attributes the action to Pilate and supplements his action with speech:

[19]Now Pilate also wrote a title and put it on the cross; it read, "Jesus of Nazareth, the King of the Jews." [20]Many of the Jews read this title, for the place where Jesus was crucified was near the city; and it was written in Hebrew, in Latin, and in Greek. [21]The chief priests of the Jews then said to Pilate, "Do not write, 'The King of the Jews,' but, 'This man says, "I am King of the Jews."'" [22]Pilate answered, "What I have written I have written." (John 19:19–22)

This account asserts that Pilate wrote the inscription of the charge and that he, rather than the soldiers, put it on the cross. In this instance, the recitation of the charge omits "this is" but identifies the victim more specifically as "Jesus of Nazareth" and asserts that the inscription contained the wording in the three major languages of the region. In the context, Johannine discourse generates an expanded chreia in which Pilate asserts that Jesus "says" that he is "King of the Jews." This expanded chreia in the Fourth Gospel stands in the context of a dialogue between Pilate and Jesus that explores the nature of Jesus' kingship (John 18:33–38); a chreia in which Jesus tells Pilate he would have no power over him unless it had been given to him from above (John 19:9–11); and two additional chreiai in which Jesus responds with kindness to his mother and the beloved disciple (19:25–27) and fulfills scripture as he cries out twice before he gives up his spirit (19:28–30) (Robbins 1988b).

In summary, there is recitation of the inscription on the cross in all four Gospels in the New Testament. In Mark, it occurs in narrational discourse that recites it as the charge against Jesus. In Matthew, the recitation occurs in the context of an action chreia that attributes the placing of the inscription on the cross to the soldiers. In Luke, the recitation occurs as a commentary on a sayings chreia that attributes mocking action and speech to the soldiers. In John, the recitation occurs in an expanded chreia that attributes the writing of the inscription and the placing of it on the cross to Pilate. In each instance, the wording in the *recitation* of the inscription varies in at least one or more ways from the three other accounts. Common to all the recitations, however, are the words "the King of the Jews."

In addition to the recitation of the inscription on the cross, Markan discourse contains an instance of recitation of a previous saying of Jesus. This occurs as follows:

And those who passed by derided him [Jesus], wagging their heads, and saying, "Aha! You who would destroy the temple and build it in three days..." (Mark 15:29)

Those passing by assert that Jesus, at some previous time, said that he would destroy the temple and rebuild it in three days. At no time in Markan discourse does Jesus ever say what the passersby attribute to him. Jesus does tell an inner group of his disciples that the temple will at some time in the future be destroyed (13:2). But he does not say that he will destroy it:

> And Jesus said to them [his disciples], "Do you not see these great buildings? There will not be left here one stone upon another, that will not be thrown down." (Mark 13:2)

Presumably God or some earthly force (like an army) will destroy the temple, not Jesus. Also, Jesus does not say that he will build the temple up in three days. But Markan discourse identifies where this "rumor" originated: some people falsely made such a claim at Jesus' trial before the high priest:

> [57]And some stood up and bore false witness against him, saying, [58]"We heard him say, 'I will destroy this temple made with hands, and in three days I will build another, not made with hands.'" (Mark 14:57–58)

In the text of Mark, then, the claim is that no "true" account of Jesus' speech contains such a saying of Jesus. It is a fascinating conundrum for interpretation, however, that Johannine discourse attributes a form of this saying to Jesus:

> Jesus answered them, "Destroy this temple, and in three days I will raise it up." (John 2:19)

Again Jesus does not assert that "he" will destroy the temple; someone, perhaps Jews themselves, will destroy it. But if and when they do, the saying asserts, Jesus will raise it up in three days. What Markan discourse claims to be "false witness" by people at Jesus' trial before the high priest, which is repeated by passersby while Jesus hangs on the cross, the Gospel of John attributes publicly to Jesus in the temple. The question regularly is: Which Gospel has it right? Since the Gospels are the only accounts of these matters available to us, it is unlikely that this question can be answered definitively. The evidence is too contradictory. A question to which the interpreter may get closer to an accurate answer is: What has happened rhetorically in early Christian discourse to create this kind of discrepancy in the tradition? For some reason, Christians spoke significantly differently from one another during the first century. Certainly anyone who has lived through the three decades of "documentaries" since the assassination of President John F. Kennedy should have no significant wonderment about the variations between the accounts of the crucifixion in the Gospels. The variation is not that surprising; rather, the challenge is to try to understand the variations using the resources for rhetorical and social analysis of language available to us.

In summary, then, there are two instances of intertextual *recitation* in the Markan account of the crucifixion. Neither is a recitation of scripture. The first is a recitation of the content of an inscription on the cross of Jesus, and the second is a recitation of a saying of Jesus that the Gospel of John attributes to Jesus in the context of his "cleansing" of the temple.

2. Recontextualization

In contrast to recitation, recontextualization presents wording from biblical texts without explicit statement or implication that the words "stand written" anywhere else. This may occur either in narration or in attributed speech. It is possible, of course, to have an explicit recitation that by virtue of its placement, attribution, or rewording has been recontextualized. The following examples present recontextualization without any indication in the text that the wording is from another text.

   a. Recontextualization in *attributed speech* occurs in John 2:16: "And he told those who sold pigeons: '*Take* these things away; you *shall not* make my Father's *house* a house of *trade.*' " Zechariah 14:21b reads: "And there shall no longer be a trader in the house of the Lord of hosts on that day." There is no indication in the Gospel of John that the words on Jesus' lips are a paraphrase of a verse from Zechariah. The result, then, is simply recontextualization of the words without any indication that they are from another text.

   b. Recontextualization in *narration* occurs in Mark 15:24:

> And they crucify him,
> and *they divide* his *garments,*
> *casting lots for* them, who would take what.

The biblical text it recontextualizes contains the following wording:

> They divided my garments among themselves,
> and for my outer garment they cast lots. (Ps 22:18 [LXX: 21:19])

The Markan recitation recontextualizes wording from the psalm, revising the tense and syntax to create a three-step statement out of parallel members (*parallelismus membrorum*; Robbins 1992b: 1176–77). The Markan text gives no indication that these words exist anywhere else in a written text. This form of writing, which significantly duplicates parts of words in a new form of sentence or clause, is characteristic of both oral and written composition in a rhetorical culture (Robbins 1991b). Significant recontextualization of wording from Psalm 22 occurs not only in Mark 15:24 but also in Mark 15:29–32, 34.

   The second instance of recontextualization in Mark 15 provides the structure and topics for the scene of the ridicule of Jesus while he hangs on the cross (15:25–32). In this instance, language from Ps 22:6–8 is recontextualized in an expanded chreia recounting this taunting of Jesus. The term "expansion" as used here comes from Theon's *Progymnasmata* (exercise 5 above). An expanded chreia amplifies either the description of the situation or the saying or both (Robbins 1988a: 17–19; 1993c: xiii–xiv; 1994b: 159–61; Mack and Robbins 1989: 17–22). Mark 15:25–32 both amplifies the description of the setting and creates multiple sayings. The verses that Mark 15:25–32 recontextualizes from the Old Testament read as follows:

> But I am a worm and not a man,
> a reproach of men and scorn of the people;
> all who have observed me sneered at me,
> they spoke with their lips, they wagged their head,
> "He hoped in the Lord, let him rescue him;
> let him save him, because he wants him." (Ps 22:6–8)

Markan narration expands these verses by dividing "all who have observed me" (Ps 22:7) into three groups:

a. ones passing by;

b. chief priests with the scribes;

c. ones crucified with him.

With this division, Markan discourse expands the discourse of the Psalm into a three-part scene.

First, the account of those passing by recontextualizes a number of words from Ps 22:7 and the word "save" from 22:8:

> And those who passed by derided him,
> *wagging their heads,*
> and *saying,*
>
>> a. "Aha, he who destroys the temple and builds it in three days;
>>
>> b. *save* yourself;
>>
>> c. come down from the cross." (Mark 15:29–30)

Second, the account of the chief priests and the scribes includes a second moment of speech that makes additional statements about being saved:

> So also the chief priests mocked him to one another with the scribes, *saying,*
>
>> a. "Others he *saved;*
>> himself he cannot *save.*" (Mark 15:31)

Third, a narrational comment about those being crucified with Jesus reformulates the statement about the sufferer as "a reproach of men" (Ps 22:6):

> And those who were crucified with him *reproached* him. (Mark 15:32)

This expansion of Ps 22:6–8 creates the middle section of the Markan account of the crucifixion.

The third instance of intertexture creates the speech in Jesus' mouth in the scene of his crying out and death (15:33–39). In this instance, Markan discourse creates a chreia directly out of Ps 22:1:

And at the ninth hour Jesus called out with a loud sound,
"Eloi, Eloi, lema sabachthani?"
which is translated, "My God, my God, why have you forsaken me?"
   (Mark 15:34)

This time an entire line of Psalm 22 is recontextualized as speech of Jesus himself. In Theon's terms (see Hock and O'Neil 1986), this is a chreia with a "commentary" that provides a translation of the Aramaic sounds (exercise 3 above).

Wording from three portions of Psalm 22 (22:18, 6–8, 1) have now become part of the account of the crucifixion of Jesus. Language that previously rehearsed the plight of a suffering righteous one is now recontextualized in the crucifixion and death of Jesus of Nazareth.

3. Reconfiguration

Reconfiguration is recounting a situation in a manner that makes the later event "new" in relation to a previous event. Because the new event is similar to a previous event, the new event replaces or "outshines" the previous event, making the previous event a "foreshadowing" of the more recent one.

We have seen above how Mark 15 recontextualizes portions of Psalm 22. A striking feature of the Markan text is the reconfiguration of scenes and statements of Psalm 22 into a scene of crucifixion. It is even more remarkable that the Markan account presents the scenes and statements from Psalm 22 in reverse order from their occurrence in the psalm. In other words, language from Ps 22:18 occurs first (Mark 15:24), from Ps 22:6–8 occurs second (Mark 15:30–31), and from Ps 22:1 occurs last (Mark 15:34). The psalm is reconfigured in such a manner that its rhetoric is reversed. Given the nature of the scenes and the content of Ps 22:1, the reversal of the order produces a reversal of the dynamics and emotions. The psalm presents a sequence in which the sufferer cries out in alienation at the beginning, experiences taunting, humiliation of nakedness, and dividing up of his garments in the middle, and expresses confidence in God at the end. The Markan account, in contrast, begins with the humiliation of nakedness, continues with taunting while he is naked, and ends with a cry of alienation. In other words, Mark 15 reconfigures an account of a suffering person who expresses hope that he will be saved into an account of a crucified person who expresses despair just before he dies (Robbins 1992b: 1178–81). Language in a psalm that moved from alienation through agony to an expression of confidence has been reconfigured into a crucifixion account that moves from agony to alienation to death. We will explore this inversion further in the section below on cultural intertexture.

4. Narrative Amplification

Extended composition containing recitation, recontextualization, and reconfiguration produces narrative amplification. Mark 15–16 presents narrative amplification of beliefs of early Christians about the death and resurrection of Jesus. The Gospel of Mark repetitively puts early Christian belief in the death and resurrection on the lips of Jesus in the form of chreiai. In the progressive texture of Mark, the first chreia expressing this belief occurs in Mark 8:31:

> And he [Jesus] began to teach them that the Son of man must suffer many things, and be rejected by the elders and chief priests and the scribes, and be killed, and after three days rise again.

This chreia on the lips of Jesus makes no reference either to burial or to appearance after resurrection. In the mouth of Jesus, this chreia focuses on suffering and rejection "by the elders, chief priests, and the scribes" prior to death and resurrection. Mark 8:31 presents Jesus as a passive victim throughout his suffering, rejection, and death. But Jesus becomes active on the third day when he "rises up." The same shift from passivity to activity occurs when Markan discourse presents two additional *recitations* of the chreia. The first recitation of the chreia after 8:31 occurs in 9:31:

> The Son of man will be handed over into the hands of men, and they will kill him; and when he is killed, after three days he will rise.

Again the shift from passivity to activity occurs when Jesus rises up. But there is an additional feature. This chreia contains language of Jesus being "handed over" to certain people who will kill him. We saw this language previously in the opening unit of Mark 15. It also appears in a third chreia that recites the death and resurrection tradition in a slightly expanded form:

> And taking the Twelve again, he began to tell them what was to happen to him, saying, "Behold, we are going up to Jerusalem; and the Son of man will be handed over to the chief priests and scribes, and they will condemn him to death, and hand him over to the Gentiles; and they will mock him, and spit upon him, and scourge him, and kill him; and after three days he will rise."

In Mark 14:43, Judas hands Jesus over to a crowd sent by the chief priests, scribes, and elders. In 14:64, the chief priests, elders, and scribes, presided over by the high priest, "condemn him as deserving death." In 15:1, the chief priests, elders, and scribes "hand over" Jesus to Pilate. In 15:15, Pilate hands Jesus over to soldiers. In 15:16–20, these Gentiles mock him, spit on him (15:19), scourge him (15:15), and kill him (15:33–39). In 16:7, the young man in a white robe in the tomb tells the three women that Jesus "has risen." With this the story ends, because with this episode Markan discourse has fully enacted the chreia as amplified narrative.

Recitation, recontextualization, and reconfiguration contribute to the narrative amplification. Reconfiguration of Psalm 22 exists in the broader context of Mark 15. Recitation of wording from Psalm 22 occurs in Mark 15:24, 29–32, 34. The recontextualization of Ps 22:18 in Mark 15:24 creates a scene in which those who crucify Jesus divide his garments among themselves. Mark 15:29–32 recontextualizes language from Ps 22:6–8 in the form of an "expansion composition" that produces a three-step scene featuring the mocking of three groups: (*a*) people passing by (15:29); (*b*) chief priests with scribes (15:31); and (*c*) the two thieves crucified alongside Jesus (15:32) (Robbins 1992b: 1177–78). Mark 15:33–39 contains recontextualization of the opening verse of Psalm 22. In this instance, the Markan text attributes the words in Aramaic to Jesus, forming a chreia statement, and to this the text adds a comment that translates the statement into Greek (Robbins 1992b: 1178). These oral-scribal activities in the context of other narration and attribution of speech create a narrative that is an extended amplification of the brief chreiai in chapters 8, 9, and 10 of Mark.

It is important to notice once again how passive Jesus is throughout the Markan account. Jesus embodies the "passivity" of the passive chreia recitations in Mark in a remarkable manner. In contrast, the Gospels of Luke and John feature Jesus actively speaking to others. The Lukan account features Jesus speaking out on four different occasions (23:28–31, 34; 23:43, 46), and the one in 23:28–31 shows significant rhetorical development (Blount 1993: 188–94). Likewise, the Johannine account features Jesus speaking at length to Pilate (18:34–37; 19:11); then he speaks in addition to his mother and the disciple whom he loved (19:26–27) and twice more (19:28, 30) while he is hanging on the cross (Robbins 1988b: 36–44). In contrast to the passive Jesus in the Markan account, Jesus is significantly active with speech in the Lukan and Johannine accounts. As we noticed in the previous chapter, Markan discourse presents Jesus as "passive" and the universe becoming passive in relation to his death. This is simply an amplified form of the abbreviated chreiai in Mark 8:31; 9:31; 10:32–34. In Markan discourse, "activity" begins in Jesus when his body is transformed into a form that can "rise up" out of the tomb. We will see yet another alternative below when we discuss elaboration in 1 Corinthians 15.

5. Thematic Elaboration

An alternative to narrative amplification is elaboration. Elaboration is not simply an expansion or amplification of a narrative. Rather, a theme or issue emerges in the form of a thesis or chreia near the beginning of a unit, and meanings and meaning-effects of this theme or issue unfold through argumentation as the unit progresses. The major topics or figures for elaborating the theme or issue are rationale, argument from the opposite, analogy, example, and authoritative testimony.

An elaboration incorporates such a wide range of resources from textual, social, and cultural traditions that ancient rhetoricians considered an elaboration to be a complete argument. We are in a fortunate position to know the view of rhetoricians contemporary with the New Testament concerning a complete argument. Therefore, we will quote two examples of a complete argument from rhetorical treatises: one from the *Rhetorica ad Herennium* and one from the *Progymnasmata* of Hermogenes. *Rhetorica ad Herennium* 2.18.28– 19.30 presents the following example of an elaboration that sets forth a complete argument:

> The most complete and perfect argument, then, is that which is comprised of five parts: the Proposition, the Reason, the Proof of the Reason, the Embellishment, and the Résumé. Through the Proposition we set forth summarily what we intend to prove. The Reason, by means of a brief explanation subjoined, sets forth the causal basis for the Proposition, establishing the truth of what we are urging. The Proof of the Reason corroborates, by means of additional arguments, the briefly presented Reason. Embellishment we use in order to adorn and enrich the argument, after the Proof has been established. The Résumé is a brief conclusion, drawing together the parts of the argument. Hence, to make the most complete use of these five parts, we shall develop an argument as follows:

> **Proposition**
> "We shall show that Ulysses had a motive in killing Ajax.

> **Rationale**
> "Indeed he wished to rid himself of his bitterest enemy, from whom, with good cause, he feared extreme danger to himself.

> **Confirmation of the Rationale**
> "He saw that, with Ajax alive, his own life would be unsafe; he hoped by the death of Ajax to secure his own safety; it was his habit to plan an enemy's destruction by whatsoever wrongful means, when he could not by rightful, as the undeserved death of Palamedes bears witness. Thus the fear of danger encouraged him to slay the man from whom he dreaded vengeance, and, in addition, the habit of wrong-doing robbed him of his scruples at undertaking the evil deed.

> **Embellishment**
> "Now not only do all men have a motive even in their least peccadilloes, but certainly they are attracted by some sure reward when they enter upon crimes which are by far the most heinous. If the hope of gaining money has led many a man to wrong-doing, if from greed for power not a few have tainted themselves with crime, if numerous men

have trafficked for a paltry profit with arrant deceit, who will find it strange that Ulysses, when under stress of acute terror, did not refrain from crime? A hero most brave, most upright, most implacable against his foes, harassed by a wrong, roused to anger — him the frightened, malevolent, guilt-conscious, guileful man wished to destroy; the treacherous man did not wish his bitter enemy to stay alive. To whom, pray, will this seem strange? For when we see wild beasts rush eagerly and resolutely to attack one another, we must not think it incredible that this creature, too — a wild, cruel, inhuman spirit — set out passionately to destroy his enemy; especially since in beasts we see no reasoning, good or bad, while he, we know, always had designs, ever so many, and ever so base.

Résumé

"If, then, I have promised to give the motive which impelled Ulysses to enter upon the crime, and if I have shown that the reckoning of a bitter enmity and the fear of danger were the factors, it must unquestionably be acknowledged that he had a motive for his crime." (*Rhetorica ad Herennium* [Cicero] 1954: 2.18.28–19.30)

This elaboration shows that a complete argument contains a rationale that supports the proposition, theme, or issue; then it contains argumentation that confirms the rationale. We noticed in the previous section that Markan discourse in chapters 15–16 was filled with rationales, with *reasons*. Since Mark 15–16 progresses in the form of narrative amplification rather than thematic elaboration, no programmatic confirmation of rationales emerges. As a result, meanings and meaning-effects remain at an implicit level. In the elaboration above, in contrast, there is argumentation that confirms the truth of the rationale. Embedded in the confirmation is an appeal to the undeserved death of Palamedes at an earlier time. This is both an argument from example and an argument from authoritative testimony from the past. These argumentative topics directly address the issues and explicitly pursue the meanings of the proposition.

After the confirmation of the rationale, the remainder of the discourse above is "embellishment." As the embellishment progresses, it uses an analogy of wild beasts to further unfold the issue and argue for the truth of the proposition and rationale at the beginning. Over a number of centuries, rhetoricians identified four major "argumentative figures" that were especially effective in confirmation and embellishment: (*a*) argument from the opposite or contrary; (*b*) argument from analogy; (*c*) argument from example; and (*d*) argument from ancient testimony. When the second-century rhetorician Hermogenes presented an elaboration of a chreia, he displayed the confirmation and embellishment as a programmatic argument from the opposite, from analogy, from example, and from authoritative testimony:

But now let us move on to the chief matter, and this is the elaboration. Accordingly, let the elaboration be as follows: (1) First, an encomium, in a few words, for the one who spoke or acted. Then (2) a paraphrase of the **chreia** itself; then (3) the rationale.

For example "Isocrates said that education's root is bitter, its fruit is sweet."

1. **Praise:** "Isocrates was wise," and you amplify the subject moderately.

2. Then the **chreia:** "He said thus and so," and you are not to express it simply but rather by amplifying the presentation.

3. Then the **rationale:** "For the most important affairs generally succeed because of toil, and once they have succeeded, they bring pleasure."

4. Then the statement from the **opposite:** "For ordinary affairs do not need toil, and they have an outcome that is entirely without pleasure; but serious affairs have the opposite outcome."

5. Then the statement from **analogy:** "For just as it is the lot of farmers to reap their fruits after working with the land, so also is it for those working with words."

6. Then the statement from **example:** "Demosthenes, after locking himself in a room and toiling long, later reaped his fruits: wreaths and public acclamations."

7. It is also possible to argue from the **statement by an authority.** For example, Hesiod said (Op. 289):

> In front of virtue gods have ordained sweat.

And another poet says (Epicharmus, Fr. 287 Kaibel):

> At the price of toil do the gods sell every good to us.

8. At the end you are to add an **exhortation** to the effect that it is necessary to heed the one who has spoken or acted.

So much for the present; you will learn the more advanced instruction later. (from Hock and O'Neil 1986: 176–77)

This display is especially important for analysis of New Testament literature because early Christian discourse attributes so much of its speech and action to specific people like Jesus, Peter, and Paul. When the discourse attributes to a specific person speech or action that pointedly raises an issue or addresses a theme, it creates a chreia, as discussed above. Hermogenes' example shows how people in the Mediterranean world were "elaborating" chreiai during the time when Christianity emerged as a particular movement within first-century Judaism.

In the example above, Hermogenes presents the theme in the form of a sayings chreia attributed to Isocrates, a fourth-century B.C.E. teacher and rhetorician. One notices how first there are statements about the speaker of the chreia that evoke the hearers' confidence that what Isocrates says is true. The possibility of "praising" the speaker of a chreia also raises the possibility of "censuring" the speaker of a chreia. This censuring will create a context in which the hearer feels confident that what the person says is false.

After Hermogenes' elaboration refers to praise and presents the chreia attributed to Isocrates, it presents a rationale to support the chreia. Then the remaining units confirm the rationale and embellish the argument. In this instance, the confirmation of the rationale takes the form of an argument from the opposite or contrary: in contrast to important affairs that generally succeed because of toil and bring pleasure, ordinary affairs do not need toil and do not bring pleasure. The embellishment then takes the form of an argument from analogy, example, and authoritative testimony (which Hermogenes calls "judgment" — that is, from a judgment made by some authoritative person; see Mack and Robbins 1989: 57–63). This example, then, helps us to see both how a theme or issue may emerge in the form of a chreia and how a confirmation and embellishment may unfold in the form of a contrary or opposite, an analogy, an example, and an authoritative testimony.

With this information, let us turn to a prime example of an argumentative elaboration about death and resurrection in early Christian discourse. It resides in the epistolary discourse of Paul in 1 Corinthians 15 (see Mack 1990; Watson 1993) and contains a thesis, rationale, confirmation of the rationale, and arguments from the contrary, from ancient testimony, from analogy, and from example. In contrast to Mark 15–16, where issues around the death and resurrection of Jesus remain implicit, 1 Corinthians 15 directly addresses the issue of the death and resurrection of Jesus and explicitly confirms and embellishes its reasoning.

The following is a paraphrase of the argument in 1 Corinthians 15 from the point of view of its presentation of a complete argument:

Theme (15:12): believers will be raised from the dead.

Rationale (15:12): because the Messiah has been raised from the dead.

Confirmation of the rationale (15:1–11): it was handed down to me that the Messiah died for our sins in accordance with the scriptures, that he was buried, that he was raised on the third day in accordance with the scriptures, and that he appeared to Cephas, the Twelve, more than five hundred brethren, James, and all the apostles. And he appeared to me also.

Argument from the contrary (15:13–19): if there is no resurrection of the dead, then the Messiah has not been raised; if the Messiah has not been raised, then our preaching is in vain and your faith is in vain, and so on.

Argument from ancient testimony (15:20–28): statements in Genesis about Adam and statements in Ps 8:6 about the Messiah having all things subject to him (including death) support the thesis that the Messiah was not held in death but has been raised from the dead.

Argument from example (15:29–34): there are believers who receive baptism for people who have died without baptism so they will be raised from the dead, and Paul himself bases his actions on the conviction that believers in the Messiah will be raised from the dead.

Argument from analogy (15:35–41): as seeds die and a new body grows up, and as there are earthly and heavenly bodies, so a person whose earthly body dies rises up as a heavenly body.

Synthesis of the argument (15:42–49): analogy that distinguishes an earthly body from a heavenly body (15:42–44) and written testimony about Adam (15:45) show the effect for believers of the raising of the Messiah from the dead (15:49).

Conclusion (15:50–58): this final section rephrases the first verse of the chapter, "Now I would remind you, brethren . . . " (15:1) into "I tell you this, brethren . . . "; establishes a relationship between the perishable and the imperishable (15:42) and those who inherit the kingdom of God (4:20; 6:9–10); uses imagery and written testimony to strengthen the convictions of the hearers that, even though resurrection of the dead appears to be a fully unbelievable thing, nevertheless this is what God has done with the Messiah and this is what he will do with believers; and ends by repeating the direct address of "brethren," reiterating praise of them as "always abounding in the work of the Lord" and "knowing that in the Lord your labor is not in vain" (15:1–2, 10–11).

Pauline discourse presents a confirmation of the rationale (15:1–11) before it presents the theme and the rationale (15:12). Then it presents the argument from the contrary, ancient testimony, example, and analogy (15:13–41). A synthesis of the argument, called in Latin a *conplexio*, precedes a conclusion to the entire chapter. As Burton Mack (1990) and Duane Watson (1993) have observed, the result is an amazing example of an intricately developed complete argument in early Christian discourse.

In the context of our ongoing analysis of Mark 15, there are a number of interesting things to observe in this argument. The confirmation of the rationale in 1 Cor 15:1–11 presents a variant tradition to the chreiai in Mark 8:31; 9:31; 10:32–34. Instead of reference to the Son of man, 1 Corinthians refers to the Messiah (Christ). Further, 1 Corinthians refers to Christ's death, burial, resurrection, and appearance. Reference to Christ's appearance is a noticeable addition to the Markan chreiai. Also, in 1 Corinthians, Jesus is a passive recipient throughout the resurrection (raised [by God]) as well as the death and burial. In 1 Corinthians, Christ overcomes passivity by appearing to many people at different times. In Mark, in contrast, Jesus rises up as the Son of man and goes before them to Galilee. If they wish to see him, they must go where he goes, for soon he will return as the Son of man. This variation means that different Christians were reasoning and arguing in various ways about issues like the death and resurrection of Jesus.

Elaboration, then, is a mode of argumentation central to early Christian discourse. Without this kind of intertextual argument, it is doubtful that Christianity would have become a powerful alternative to other Jewish groups at the time. Mark 15:1–16:8 does not contain this mode of elaboration. Rather, it presents narrative amplification. Storytelling has its own rhetorical power. Working side by side, thematic elaboration and narrative amplification are effective means to communicate the worldview of a religious movement.

Oral-scribal intertexture, then, concerns recitation, recontextualization, reconfiguration, narrative amplification, and elaboration. All of these are ways of reworking specific traditions that are handed on by word of mouth or written text. Reworking more general traditions takes us to cultural intertexture, which is the topic of the next section.

B. Cultural Intertexture

In addition to their interactive relation to other texts, texts have an interactive relation to cultures of various kinds. Cultural knowledge is "insider" knowledge. This kind of knowledge is known only by people inside a particular culture or by people who have learned about that culture through some kind of interaction with it — either vicariously in a context of education or in a context of direct interaction with members of it.

Cultural intertexture appears in word and concept patterns and configurations; values, scripts, codes, or systems (e.g., purity, law, covenant); and myths (e.g., wisdom, Oedipus, Hermes). Cultural intertexture appears in a text either through reference or allusion and echo.

1. *Reference or allusion:* A *reference* is a word or phrase that points to a personage or tradition known to people on the basis of tradition. An interpreter will be able to find various texts that exhibit meanings associated with a reference. An *allusion* is a statement that presupposes a tradition that exists in textual form, but the text being interpreted is not attempting to "recite" the text. With both reference and allusion, the text interacts with phrases, concepts, and traditions that are "cultural" possessions that anyone who knows a particular culture may use.

Good examples of cultural reference and cultural allusion occur in Luke 1:68–69. Both "a horn of salvation" and "the house of his servant David" are references in these verses that evoke cultural intertexture. What do they mean? Only people who have been raised in Jewish culture or have been educated in it as an "other" culture will know their meanings. The phrase "a horn of salvation" appears in 1 Sam 2:10; Ps 18:2; and Ps 132:17, alluding to a Davidic ruler who will have power. These texts do not, however, also refer to "the house of David." Rather, 2 Sam 7:1–17 contains an oracle by Nathan to David that refers twice to David as "servant" (2 Sam 7:5, 9) and presents the word of the Lord as saying: "The Lord will make you a house…;" and "Your house and your kingdom shall be made sure forever…" (2 Sam 7:11, 16). All of these texts exhibit the existence of a cultural tradition to which Luke 1:68–69 makes reference. In addition, 2 Sam 7:12 says: "I will raise up your offspring after you." The presence of "he has raised up a horn of salvation" in Luke 1:69 makes this an allusion to Nathan's oracle that is the story of the "initial promise" that God would establish the "throne" of the royal dynasty of David "forever."

Another instance of cultural reference occurs in Acts 14:11–12 when the people of Lystra, speaking in Lycaonian, refer to Barnabas and Paul as Zeus and Hermes who have "come down to us in the likeness of men." Persons know the meaning of Zeus and Hermes only if they have Greek cultural knowledge. There is, however, more than a "reference" to these two Greek gods in this text. Acts 14:11 refers to their coming down to earth in the like- ness of men. Is there an allusion here to one or more stories that recount a time when one or both of these gods came down to earth? Interpreters reg- ularly raise the possibility that the verse in Acts alludes to the story of the visit of the gods Zeus and Hermes to the elderly couple Baucis and Philemon in Ovid's *Metamorphoses* 8:611–724 (Conzelmann 1987: 110; Johnson 1992: 248). Recently, Amy Wordelman has presented evidence that readers under- stand the dynamics of the Lukan episode only if they have knowledge of the tradition of Zeus's visit to King Lycaon (see Ovid *Metamorphoses* 1.226–61; Apollodorus *Library* 3.8.1; Wordelman 1993: 226–31). If this is true, Acts 14:11–12 contains cultural allusion to a particular episode in addition to cultural reference to these two Greek gods.

In summary, references and allusions do not "recite" any actual text of a story, nor do they recontextualize, reconfigure, elaborate, or amplify it. Ref- erences simply "point" to a personage, concept, or tradition, and allusions "interact" with cultural concepts or traditions. Various texts rather than one text lie in the background, with the result that interpreters regularly may dis- agree over whether or not a particular text lies in the background. If there is no disagreement, the nature of the intertexture is oral-scribal rather than cul- tural. References and allusions may occur in completely oral culture, namely, where nothing but "oral text" exists, and they are also common in rhetori- cal culture, namely, a culture where oral speech and written texts continually interact with one another (Robbins 1994c). New Testament discourse contains references and allusions to people, gods, and traditions in Jewish and Greco-Roman culture.

2. *Echo*. An "echo" is a word or phrase that evokes, or potentially evokes, a concept from cultural tradition. In other words, echo does not contain either a word or phrase that is "indisputably" from only one cultural tradition. Echo is subtle and indirect. One person may hear it while another does not, and the speaker may or may not have directly intended the echo to be there. The result is that interpreters regularly will debate the presence or absence of a particular echo in the text under consideration.

An important argument for the existence of echo in a chapter of New Testament text has been Burton L. Mack's analysis of the use of *paideia* (instruction on how to live a successful life according to the values of Greek society) in Mark 4:1–34, the text on the planting of seeds. Mack presents the following Greek and Latin texts to support his case:

> The views of our teachers are as it were the seeds. Learning from childhood is analogous to the seeds falling betimes upon the prepared ground. (Hippocrates 3)

> As is the seed that is ploughed into the ground, so must one expect the harvest to be, and similarly when good education is ploughed into young persons, its effect lives and burgeons throughout their lives, and neither rain nor drought can destroy it. (Antiphon frag. 60)

> Words should be scattered like seed; no matter how small the seed may be, if it once has found favorable ground, it unfolds its strength and from an insignificant thing spreads to its greatest growth. (Seneca *Epistles* 38.2)

> If you wish to argue that the mind requires cultivation, you would use a comparison drawn from the soil, which if neglected produces thorns and thickets, but if cultivated will bear fruit. (Quintilian 5.11.24) (Mack and Robbins 1989: 155–56; Mack 1988: 159–60)

Again, interpreters regularly may disagree over the presence or absence of cultural echo in a text. No single text undeniably lies in the background to negotiate the dispute. The echo of *paideia* in Mark 4 represents the kind of cultural intertexture Abraham J. Malherbe has exhibited in 1 Corinthians 8–9 with the relation of Pauline discourse to both Hellenistic-Jewish and Greco-Roman moral philosophical discourse (Malherbe 1995; cf. 1987, 1989).

Returning now to Mark 15, let us look for cultural intertexture. Since there are multiple cultural dimensions in any substantive text, it is not possible to pursue anything that approaches a comprehensive survey. We will, therefore, limit ourselves to an interesting example. A short span of text in

Dio Chrysostom exhibits an intriguing aspect of cultural intertexture. The text reads as follows:

> They [the Persians at the Sacian festival] take one of their prisoners who has been condemned to death, set him on the king's throne, give him the royal apparel, and permit him to give orders, to drink and carouse, and to dally with the royal concubines during those days, and no one prevents his doing anything he pleases. After that they strip and scourge him and then hang him.... If [the prisoner] understands [the meaning of the action], he probably breaks out into wailing and refuses to go along without protesting. (Dio Chrysostom *Discourses* 4.67, 69)

The close relation between the Markan scenes and the actions in the ritual of the Sacian festival in the eastern Mediterranean suggests the interaction of two major cultural intertextures in the Markan account. Not only is the Markan crucifixion a manifestation of the experiences of a suffering righteous one according to Jewish tradition; it is a manifestation of a Mediterranean cultural ritual in which the humiliation of a prisoner mocks the role and activities of a king. The Markan account of the crucifixion of Jesus, which may be the earliest Christian account available to us, is a reconfiguration of Jewish and Mediterranean cultural traditions that distinctively merges the experiences of the final days of the suffering righteous person with the public humiliation that arises from being ironically associated with the role and activities of a king. The Messiah of Israel in Christian discourse is neither the traditional sufferer nor the traditional king. The meaning-effects of the drama reverberate across cultural boundaries. The Christian Messiah is bicultural or multicultural in his manifestation of personal, social, cultural, and religious attributes. The unusual features of the drama emerge in the role of Barabbas, which provides a distinctive form of irony for the story, and the burial of the corpse, which provides the context for the empty tomb.

The irony, from the perspective of Mediterranean cultural logic, is that those things that are done to Jesus are the things "customarily" done to the one whom an official "releases to the people" at the time of their festival. In the Markan account, the "son of the Father" (Barabbas), who was a murderous revolutionary, was "released" to disappear from the events of history, while one who was "not released" was put through "the customary ritual" of mockery and crucifixion as though he were a released prisoner appropriately being mocked as a king to renew everyone's awareness of the responsibilities of a true king, who is a son of Zeus (Robbins 1992a: 187–91; 1992b: 1172–75).

It is a remarkable symptom of the cross-cultural manifestation of actions and configurations in the Markan account that the sequence of scenes in Mark 15 follows the sequence of the Dio Chrysostom text, and this produces a reversal of the order of scenes in Psalm 22. The oral-scribal intertexture of Psalm 22 does not simply complement the multicultural intertexture of the humiliated, righteous king. Rather, the rhetoric of Psalm 22 is in many ways subservient to the rhetoric of this new cultural configuration. Jesus' cry of desperation and alienation at the last moment of breath is a cross-cultural manifestation of the suffering and humiliation of a leader chosen by the gods and the people in the Mediterranean world. The cultural intertexture of the account refigures both Jewish tradition and Hellenistic-Roman tradition. Is Jesus a particular kind of Jewish king or a particular kind of Hellenistic-Roman king? Is Jesus a particular kind of Jewish savior or a particular kind of Hellenistic-Roman savior? The interplay of Jewish and Hellenistic-Roman expectations, actions, and meaning-effects transcends traditional configurations in both cultural contexts. This Markan discourse is a distinctive formulation that challenges other Mediterranean portrayals of a personage who lives an exemplary life and dies an exemplary death for the benefit of humans.

C. Social Intertexture

Social knowledge is commonly held by all persons of a region, no matter what their particular "cultural" location may be. In general, social knowledge is visible. One obtains it by observing the behavior and public material objects produced by other people. In other words, social knowledge is readily accessible to all people through general interaction, in contrast to cultural knowledge, which must be taught with careful use of language and transmission of specific traditions. Social knowledge falls generally into the four following categories:

   a. *social role* (soldier, shepherd, slave, athlete) or *social identity* (Greek, Roman, Jew);

   b. *social institution* (empire, synagogue, trade workers' association, household);

   c. *social code* (e.g., honor, hospitality);

   d. *social relationship* (patron, friend, enemy, kin).

In Mark 15, social roles or identities appear with the chief priests, elders, and scribes (15:1, 3, 11, 31), a prisoner (15:6), an insurrectionist (15:7), a murderer (15:7), a king (15:9, 12, 18, 26, 32), Jews (15:9, 12, 18), soldiers (15:16), a Cyrenian (15:21), bandit-robbers (15:27), and a centurion (15:39, 44–45). The narration does not designate the social identity of Pilate (15:1–15, 43–45), but research outside of the Gospel of Mark indicates that he was a Roman prefect (Vardaman 1962).

Social institutions appear with the council (15:1), the battalion of soldiers (15:16), and the temple (15:38). Crucifixion is a practice of the Roman government as an institution, adopted from the Carthaginians during the Punic Wars (Hengel 1977).

Social codes appear in terms of honor throughout the chapter. Country in relation to city appears in 15:21. Gender is an issue with the appearance of the women in 15:40–41. (For an exploration of these codes, see the discussion of social and cultural texture below.)

Social relationships appear in the form of enemies (15:11–14), kinship (father and sons: 15:21; mother and sons: 15:40), and friends (15:40–41, 43–46, 47).

All of these phenomena in the text raise the issue of social meanings that interpreters investigate by means of data outside the Gospel of Mark. Meanings of these social roles, identities, institutions, codes, and relationships are appropriately explored with the aid of texts, inscriptions, archaeological data, sculpture, paintings, and so on outside the Markan text. These phenomena, then, provide a rich social intertexture for the discourse of the Gospel of Mark. Research in social phenomena outside Mark sheds important light on the nature of this social intertexture.

Cultural rather than social intertexture appears in references to the Passover festival (15:6), the Messiah (15:32), God (15:34), the son of God (15:39), the day of preparation (15:42), the sabbath (15:42), and the kingdom of God (15:43). The meanings of these phenomena require detailed exploration of Jewish texts, since they are products of Jewish culture.

D. Historical Intertexture

Historical intertexture concerns events that have occurred at specific times in specific locations. The term "historical" is commonly used in a manner that does not discriminate between historical, social, and cultural phenomena. This leads to imprecision in analysis, interpretation, explanation, and understanding. In socio-rhetorical criticism, the term "historical" is used with reference to events. Social (which includes political and economic) and cultural phenomena are integral to historical events. "Interpreting" a historical event requires knowledge of social, cultural, and ideological phenomena operative in it.

I. Multiplicity of the Data

There is always a limited amount of information about a historical event. When analyzing the historical intertexture of a text, one of the issues is if this is the only information about the event or whether there are other accounts not dependent on this textual account. The nature of the historical intertexture in any text, therefore, may fall into one of the following categories:

  a. It is the only information about an event. In other words, this is the only existing data to support a claim that this event occurred. Belief that the information is reliable is a matter of trust because there is no other independent confirmation of the event.

b. All the accounts of an event that exist appear to be dependent on one another. In other words, there are no clearly "independent" accounts of the same event; all of the information comes from a "common" source.

c. The independent accounts agree on the basic issues.

d. The independent accounts contain significant disagreements.

2. Nature of the Data

Different kinds of data are the basis for historical information. Interpreters regularly place a higher trust in records of various kinds than in literary accounts, which have a wide range of rhetorical interests. Analysis of historical intertexture, therefore, calls for an awareness of the nature of the data the interpreter has available. This yields the following spectrum of data for analysis and interpretation of historical intertexture:

a. Historical inscriptions, records, annals, and so on

b. Literary discourse

    1. Literary narration
John 20:11: "But Mary stood weeping outside the tomb, and as she wept she stooped to look into the tomb; and she saw two angels in white, sitting where the body of Jesus had lain, one at the head and one at the feet."

    2. Epistolary discourse
1 Cor 2:1: "When I came to you, brethren, I did not come proclaiming to you the testimony of God in lofty words or wisdom. For I decided to know nothing among you except Jesus Christ and him crucified."

    3. Speech of a character in a narrative
Acts 22:4–5: "I persecuted this Way to the death, binding and delivering in prison both men and women, as the high priest and the whole council of elders bear me witness."

Since the nature of narrative discourse is to claim to be true "historically," it is important to gain some insight on both the amount of information and the nature of the data available for an assessment of historical intertexture in Mark 15. In other words, there are many assertions in Markan discourse that imply the existence of a historical fact, event, or custom outside of the text, and we need to have a close look at them. One of the keys to historical conclusions is the precise formulation of appropriate questions. An interpreter often can decide how to formulate good questions by ascertaining aspects of the narrative that appear to be plausible or implausible. The following list exhibits some aspects of the historical intertexture of Mark 15:1–46:

PEOPLE, PLACES, AND INSTITUTIONS

A. Positive evidence outside of Christian sources

> 1a. a man named Pilate with political and legal power in Jerusalem (15:1)

> 2a. a Sanhedrin in Jerusalem constituted by chief priests, scribes, elders (15:1)

> 3a. a place in Jerusalem named Golgotha (15:22)

B. No evidence outside of Christian sources

> 3b. a place named Golgotha as a place of crucifixion (15:22)

> 4. an insurrectionist named Barabbas (15:7)

> 5. a man named Simon of Cyrene, father of Alexander and Rufus (15:21)

> 6. a respected member of the Jerusalem council named Joseph of Arimathea (15:43)

EVENTS

A. Positive evidence outside of Christian sources

> 1b. death of Jesus of Nazareth occurred by crucifixion while Pilate was prefect (15:24)

B. No evidence outside of Christian sources

> 7. splitting of the curtain of the temple from top to bottom (15:38)

> 8a. Pilate's releasing of an insurrectionist prisoner at a festival (15:6)

> 9a. an insurrection just before Passover on the year of Jesus' death (15:7)

> 10a. an inscription of the charge on Jesus' cross (15:26)

> 11a. crucifixion of two bandits alongside Jesus (15:27)

C. Historically implausible

> 2b/12. a meeting of the Sanhedrin early in the morning of Passover Day (15:1)

> 13. an eclipse of the sun from noon to 3 P.M. on the day of Jesus' crucifixion (15:33)

> 14a. wrapping Jesus' corpse in a linen shroud (15:46)

CUSTOMS

  A. Positive evidence outside of Christian sources

     8b. releasing a prisoner at the time of a festival (15:6)

     9b. insurrections in Jerusalem in which people were imprisoned (15:7)

    10b. an inscription of the charge on a cross (15:26)

    11b. crucifixion of more than one person at a time (15:27)

    14b. wrapping a corpse in strips of cloth (not a large linen shroud) (15:46)

    15. laying a corpse in a tomb hewn out of rock and rolling a stone against the opening of the tomb (15:46)

  B. Historically implausible

    8c. a custom of Pilate releasing a prisoner each year at the Jewish festival of Passover (15:6)

First (1a, b), no one questions the existence of a man named Pontius Pilate. Historical investigation has yielded extensive evidence that Pontius Pilate was the prefect (*praefectus*) of Judea from 26 until 37 C.E., with his headquarters in Caesarea Maritima. A Latin inscription discovered in Caesarea in 1961 verifies that his official title was prefect rather than procurator, which is the title Tacitus (*Annals* 15.44.33) and, in Greek (*epitropos*), both Philo (*Embassy to Gaius* 299) and Josephus (*Wars* 2.169) assigned to him. When Pilate visited Jerusalem, he resided either in the palace of Herod the Great or, perhaps preferably, in the fortress of Antonia on the north side of the temple court. Philo of Alexandria (*Embassy to Gaius* 38) quotes a letter from Agrippa I to Caligula that describes Pilate as "inflexible, merciless, and obstinate" and gives a catalogue of his crimes and excesses (cf. Josephus *Wars* 2.14.8). Pilate had the power to delegate activities to soldiers who were in his charge. Tacitus (*Annals* 15.44, and perhaps Josephus) records that Jesus was killed while Pilate held his office.

Second (2a, b), there was a Sanhedrin in Jerusalem. Possibly it comprised seventy-one members during the 30s C.E. The high priest served as its president, and heads of the great priestly families (chief priests), scribes, and lay leaders (elders) were members of it (Schürer 1973: 2.1.163–95). It is highly unlikely that an emergency meeting of the entire Sanhedrin could have been convened early in the morning of Passover Day.

Third (3a, b), Golgotha is known in Jewish legend as the place of the burial of Adam's skull (Taylor 1963: 488). The location of Golgotha comes from later Christian sources that identify it on the site of the Church of the Holy Sepulcher. There is no extra-Christian evidence that it was a place where people were crucified.

Fourth (4), there is no corroborative evidence outside of Christian Gospels of an insurrectionist named Barabbas. The name looks suspicious because it means, in Aramaic, "son of the Father." On the other hand, the Talmud refers to rabbis with the names R. Samuel Bar Abba and R. Nathan Bar Abba (Taylor 1963: 581).

Fifth (5), there is no evidence of Simon of Cyrene outside of Christian sources. A man named Rufus is mentioned in Rom 16:13. There is no evidence that this Rufus was the son of Simon. It was, in fact, customary for each man to carry his own cross beam (*patibulum*; Plutarch *De Sera Numinis Vindicta* 2.554A; Taylor 1963: 587), as John 19:31 presents the account.

Sixth (6), there is no evidence, outside of Christian texts, about Joseph of Arimathea either as a person or as a member of the Jerusalem council.

Seventh (7), there is no corroborative evidence of a split in either the inner or the outer curtain of the Jerusalem temple in the early 30s C.E.

Eighth (8a, b, c), there is no record outside of Christian sources that Pilate regularly or ever released a prisoner at the time of the Passover festival or any other festival in the realm of his jurisdiction. Moreover, the accounts of the severity with which he governed suggest that such an act, under any circumstances, would be highly unlikely. There is, on the other hand, evidence that legates and prefects, at times, did release prisoners.

Ninth (9a, b), while there is positive evidence that Passover was a time of concern for Roman prefects, because of the potential for insurrection or general tumult, there is no evidence outside Christian sources for an insurrection prior to Passover during the early 30s C.E. (Taylor 1963: 581).

Tenth (10a, b), there is evidence that an inscription of the crime often was placed on a cross above the head of the crucified person (Lane 1974: 568; Juvenal *Satires* 6.230; Pliny the Younger *Epistles* 6.10.3; 9.19.3; Suetonius *Life of Caligula* 32; *Life of Domitian* 10). There is no corroboration of this exact inscription on Jesus' cross outside of Christian sources. Many scholars consider the existence of an inscription to be "solid historical fact" (Lane 1974: 568).

Eleventh (11a, b), regularly more than one person was crucified at a time. Therefore, it would be historically plausible that additional people would be crucified along with Jesus. To have two people, one on the right and one on the left, crucified with Jesus looks schematized, however. This phenomenon would appear to derive from a concept of mockery of him as a pseudo-king: both his "right-hand" and "left-hand" associates are "bandit-revolutionaries."

Twelfth (12), specialists in the legal-political aspects of political leadership in Jerusalem during the second and third decades of the first century consider it highly unlikely that an emergency session of the council and/or sanhedrin could be convened on the morning of Passover day.

Thirteenth (13), an eclipse is impossible at the time of the full moon, which it would have been at the beginning of Passover, as Origen pointed out (Taylor 1963: 593). If some phenomenon caused darkness, it would have had to be something like dark clouds.

Fourteenth (14a, b), corpses were often wrapped in cloth strips before they were placed in tombs, not in a sheet large enough to wrap around the entire body.

Fifteenth (15), bodies of crucified people regularly were left on the cross until birds had picked most of the flesh away. Regularly, also, no one including the family was allowed to take the body down and give it a proper burial. A regular way to give a body a proper burial would be to wash it, wrap it tightly in cloth strips, and lay it on a slab of rock above ground until it decomposed. Then the bones would be put underneath the slab, along with the bones of previous bodies that had decomposed on the slab, so someone else's body could be laid on the slab.

One can see that the discourse in this chapter is replete with historical intertexture. One can also see how historical scholarship could establish dominance over the interpretation of a chapter like this. The chapter raises many interesting historical issues, and the pursuit of those issues is important, challenging, and fascinating.

Conclusion

Oral-scribal, cultural, social, and historical intertexture are integral aspects of any richly textured text. Texts like Mark 15 and 1 Corinthians 15 contain an almost unlimited number of intertextual dimensions. For this reason, they can always be compared with another text or another tradition, even if these traditions have no specific relation to first-century Mediterranean culture.

STUDY GUIDE:
Oral-Scribal, Historical, and Social Intertexture — Use of the Old Testament in Acts 2

NOTE: This guide is based on the New Revised Standard Version.

During the time of the early church, various groups were involved in interpretation of the Hebrew Scriptures — those writings Christians eventually called the Old Testament. Around 150 c.e., an early Christian named Justin Martyr wrote a long essay entitled "A Dialogue with Trypho (the Jew)" that discussed the differences between Christian and Jewish interpretations of the scriptures. Even within Judaism, various groups (such as the Essenes) produced their own interpretations. The varying interpretations help us to distinguish between various Jewish groups at that time (of which Christianity was one). This study guide is designed to lead us toward careful and thorough analysis of the method of interpretation called "fulfillment of prophecy," which was often used by early Christians.

"The scriptures" for earliest Christianity (30–140 C.E.) were the Hebrew Scriptures in Greek translation (called the Septuagint [LXX]). During those years, however, Christians were writing new pieces of literature, and historians know the wording of about sixty of them. From those sixty pieces, twenty-seven documents became particularly popular and were eventually chosen as "additional scripture" (new authoritative writings) to be added to the Hebrew Scriptures. These became known as the "New Covenant" or "New Testament." The twenty-seven documents are listed by Bishop Athanasius in a letter written in 367 C.E. These particular twenty-seven documents have influenced Christianity in a special way; selection of some of the other documents could have resulted in quite a different kind of Christianity.

When the Acts of the Apostles was written (about 85 C.E.), this new body of literature had not yet been compiled. Thus, the author of Acts draws on the Hebrew Scriptures and interprets them using the "fulfillment of prophecy" method. In this study guide we will examine some interpretations that are made in the second chapter of Acts.

•

1. Read the first two chapters of the Acts of the Apostles to become familiar with the *historical intertexture* called forth by the narration.

2. Now look at Acts 2:16. Verse 16 introduces a *recitation* of five verses from the prophetic book of Joel in the Old Testament. Find out where the *scribal intertext* is in Joel (you find this by looking at the note on verse 17 at the bottom of the page). Now look the passage up in the Old Testament. Compare Acts 2:17 with the *intertext* in Joel. Do you agree that Acts 2:17 *recites exact words of another written text* "with some additions and changes"? Explain the change from "then afterward" in Joel 2 to "in the last days it will be" in Acts 2. Explain the addition of "God declares" in the first line in Acts 2:17. Look around in the text of Joel before you give an answer. Especially, see Joel 2:19. The Greek wording of "in the last days" contains the adjective *eschatos*, from which we get "eschatology" — the doctrine of the last or final things that will happen in the world. Do you think the author of Acts, or Peter, has the right to change the Old Testament in this way when he leads us to think he is *reciting* it exactly? Why or why not?

3. Now compare Acts 2:18 with Joel 2:29. Basically this is *recitation of exact words of another written text,* but again there is a noticeable addition. Can you explain why some member of the Christian community added the extra clause? What does 1 Cor 11:5 suggest to you about the *social intertexture* of Acts 2:18 — namely, accepted social activity by women in the Christian community? Could this be the reason for the expansion of this verse?

4. Now compare Acts 2:19–21 with Joel 2. You will notice a distinction in

Acts between "portents" in the heavens "above" and "signs" on the earth "be-low," emphasizing spatial distinction between things above and things below and the different nature of actions there and here. Notice the *recontextual-ization* of Joel 2:28, "I will pour out my Spirit upon all flesh" in Acts 2:33. Who is "the Lord" in Joel 2:31–32? Who is "the Lord" in Acts 2:20–21? Acts 2:21 *omits words* from Joel 2:32 by failing to *recite* a large portion of the verse. Explain why Christians would omit the final part of the verse.

5. Now turn to Psalm 16 in the Old Testament and read it entirely through. About whom, according to the title under "Psalm 16," does the psalmist speak and pray? In other words, who is saying "my" and "me" in the following verses?

> ⁹Therefore my heart is glad,
>   and my soul rejoices;
>   my body also rests secure.
> ¹⁰For you do not give me up to Sheol,
>   or let your faithful one see the Pit.

Who is "your faithful one" in verse 10? What do the notes at the bottom of the page say about the psalmist, Sheol, and Pit? Read the additional note to which the note to verse 10 refers, and read the additional passages to which the note to Ps 6:5 refers.

6. Now read Acts 2:22–31. Read the first part of 2:25 very carefully. Who are "I," "the Lord," "me," and "he" in the *scribal recitation* in Acts 2:25? In your opinion, is there ambiguity in the text itself, or are the referents per-fectly clear? Notice the *recontextualization* of the psalm in Acts 2:29–32. On the basis of verses 27 and 31, who is now understood to be "your Holy [or "faithful"] one"?

7. Do you sense that Acts 2 *reconfigures* the meaning of Psalm 16 by *recon-textualizing* it? Why do you think the early Christian community reconfigured the meaning of this psalm?

8. Read Ps 110:1. On the basis of the notes, what kind of person wrote this psalm, and to whom was he referring with the first "the Lord" and the second "my lord"? Read Acts 2:32–35 and compare the *recitation* in 2:34–35 with Ps 110:1. According to the author of Acts, who wrote the psalm? For the author of Acts, who is the first "the Lord" and who is the second "my Lord"? Has a change in wording occurred? Has a *reconfiguration* of the meaning occurred? Is the *reconfiguration* significant? Notice the concluding statement in Acts 2:36.

Chapter 3 _____

Social and Cultural Texture

LIVING WITH A TEXT IN THE WORLD

Analysis of the social and cultural texture of a text takes interpreters into sociological and anthropological theory. The issue here is not simply the intertexture of a text but its social and cultural nature *as* a text. What kind of a social and cultural person would anyone be who lives in the "world" of a particular text? Investigation of the social and cultural texture of a text includes exploring the social and cultural "location" of the language and the type of social and cultural world the language evokes or creates.

The social and cultural texture of a text emerges in specific social topics, common social and cultural topics, and final cultural categories. Specific social topics in the text reveal the religious responses to the world in its discourse. Do the narrator and characters in the story assert or imply that the world is evil, and if so how evil is it? Do they indicate how the world could be changed? If the world cannot be changed, do they indicate how it is possible to live in it without participating in evil? Answers to these questions lie in specific topics of discussion that characterize the nature of the world and what it is necessary to do to live in it or to change it. Common social and cultural topics in the text exhibit the overall perception in the text of the context in which people live in the world. These topics exhibit broad insights about systems of exchange and benefit. The social and cultural systems presupposed in the text may be significantly distinct from the social and cultural systems in which the interpreter himself or herself lives. Analysis and interpretation of the common social and cultural topics in a text may take an interpreter beyond his or her own presuppositions into the foreign social and cultural world of the text. When this happens, a deeper level of the social and cultural texture of the text begins to emerge as well as a clearer understanding of implications in the text about living a committed religious life in the world. Final cultural categories in the text show the priorities in the text's discourse among topics like what constitutes being lawful, expedient, holy, valiant, and so on. Since people in different cultural contexts negotiate these priorities differently, analysis and interpretation of them reveal cultural location and orientation toward other cultures in the discourse. Analysis and interpretation of this location and orientation reveal a fuller understanding of topics that do and do not appear, and they carry implications for the kind of culture the discourse naturally nurtures among readers who take its discourse seriously. Together, then, specific social topics, common social and cultural topics, and final cultural categories exhibit the social and cultural texture of a text and reveal the potential of the text to encourage its readers to adopt certain social and cultural locations and orientations rather than others.

A. Specific Social Topics

Texts with a substantive religious texture contain specific ways of talking about the world. The topics of interest and concern in any one religious text may establish a relation to the world significantly different from another text. Richard Niebuhr's *Christ and Culture* was an earlier attempt to identify the relation of major sectors of Christianity to the world. Bryan Wilson's typology of sects, based on a cross-cultural spectrum of religious groups, has established a much more broadly based approach, organizing data from a wide variety of religious groups in a taxonomy of seven kinds of religious responses to the world. In the terms of an anthropologist like Clifford Geertz, each kind of response creates a kind of culture that gives meanings, values, traditions, convictions, rituals, beliefs, and actions to people. Applying this taxonomy to New Testament literature reveals the kinds of cultures earliest Christianity nurtured and maintained in the first-century Mediterranean world. It also suggests to us what kind of Christian cultures this literature has the potential to nurture in modern society. As an interpreter approaches New Testament literature, each kind of social response appears as a type of social rhetoric. The seven types are as follows (much of the following is verbatim wording from Wilson 1963, 1969, 1973: 22–26; see Wilde 1978).

1. Conversionist

The conversionist response is characterized by a view that the world is corrupt because people are corrupt. If people can be changed, the world will be changed. Salvation is considered to be available not through objective agencies but only by a profound and supernaturally wrought transformation of the self. The world itself will not change, but the presence of a new subjective orientation to it will itself be salvation.

2. Revolutionist

The revolutionist response declares that only the destruction of the world — the natural world but also, more specifically, the social order — will be sufficient to save people. Supernatural powers must perform the destruction because people lack the power if not to destroy the world then certainly to re-create it. Believers may themselves feel called upon to participate in the process of overturning the world, but they know that they do no more than assist greater powers and give a testimony of faith by their words and deeds.

3. Introversionist

The introversionist response views the world as irredeemably evil and considers salvation to be attainable only by the fullest possible withdrawal from it. The self may be purified by renouncing the world and leaving it. This might be an individual response, of course, but as the response of a social movement it leads to the establishment of a separated community preoccupied with its own holiness and its means of insulation from the wider society.

4. Gnostic-Manipulationist

The gnostic-manipulationist response seeks only a transformed set of relationships — a transformed method of coping with evil. Whereas the foregoing orientations reject the goals of society as well as the institutionalized means of attaining them and the existing facilities by which people might be saved, the gnostic-manipulationist rejects only the means and the facilities. Salvation is possible in the world, and evil may be overcome if people learn the right means, improved techniques, to deal with their problems.

5. Thaumaturgical

The thaumaturgical response focuses on the individual's concern for relief from present and specific ills by special dispensations. The request for supernatural help is personal and local, and its operation is magical. Salvation is immediate but has no general application beyond the given case and others like it. Salvation takes the form of healing, assuagement of grief, restoration after loss, reassurance, the foresight and avoidance of calamity, and the guarantee of eternal (or at least continuing) life after death.

6. Reformist

The reformist response views the world as corrupt because its social structures are corrupt. If the structures can be changed so that the behaviors they sanction are changed, then salvation will be present in the world. This response, then, assumes that evil may be dealt with according to supernaturally given insights about the ways in which social organization should be amended. Investigation of the ways of the world and recommendations for amending it are the essential orientation. The specific alterations to be made are revealed to people whose hearts and minds are open to supernatural influence.

7. Utopian

The utopian response seeks to reconstruct the entire social world according to divinely given principles, rather than simply to amend it from a reformist position. The goal of a utopian response is to establish a new social organization that will eliminate evil. It is much more radical than the reformist response because it insists on complete replacement of the present social organization. The utopian response differs from the revolutionist response by insisting that people themselves remake the world rather than that a divine power destroy this present world and re-create another. In turn, a utopian response is more active and constructive than an introversionist response of simply withdrawing from the world.

•

The Gospel of Mark contains substantive thaumaturgical and revolutionist discourse (see Wilde 1978: 61). Thaumaturgical discourse occurs in "summaries of thaumaturgical activity in 1:32–34, 39; 3:10; 6:5, 12–13, 30, 53–56" and in "twenty thaumaturgical acts" that are "local, individual, specific, and for the present time." This means that the discourse in Mark evokes an attraction to "the present, pragmatic comfort" of healing similar to "many pentecostals, charismatics and other religious healers" in our own time (Wilde 1978: 55). Yet thaumaturgical discourse in Mark is embedded in revolutionist discourse. The power of God will bring the fullest form of its benefits when it causes the sun and moon to become dark, the stars and powers in the heavens to lose their powers, and the Son of man to gather the elect "from the four winds, from the extremity of the earth to the extremity of heaven" (13:24–27). Then heaven and earth will pass away (13:31). The discourse presents no vision of a new creation. Rather, it simply speaks of the Son of man gathering the elect, and the implication is that this is an action by which he takes them into "eternal life" in an "age to come" (10:30; see Wilde 1978: 59–61).

In the context of these dominant forms of discourse, the Gospel of Mark contains a few assertions that could evoke a utopian response (10:42–45; 11:17; Wilde 1978: 51–52), a reformist response (6:11; 12:9; 13:10; Wilde 1978: 52), an introversionist response (1:3–5, 12–13, 35, 45; 6:31–32, 35; Wilde 1978: 52–53), or a conversionist response that focuses on repentance (1:4, 15; 6:12), faith (2:5; 5:34; 9:23; 10:52; 11:22–24; 15:32), or love (12:30–31; Wilde 1978: 56–59). These assertions are simply occasional, however, and embedded in contexts where topics concerning the thaumaturgical and revolutionist powers of God dominate the discourse. Therefore, they do not become central social modes of response to the world in the text.

In addition, however, a significant amount of gnostic-manipulationist discourse occurs in the Gospel of Mark (Robbins 1994a: 74–81). Not only does Jesus speak "in parables" (3:23; 4:2, 10, 13, 30, 33, 34; 7:17; 12:1, 12; 13:28), but "everything happens" in parables (4:11). In accord with this emphasis, parables and many significant events in Mark are puzzling, enigmatic, unclear, and mysterious. These emphases are characteristic of gnostic-manipulationist discourse. People must see and take heed, but true understanding is hidden (4:22) and not clear even to the inner circle of Jesus' followers (4:9, 12; 7:14; 8:17, 21). In the midst of thaumaturgical and revolutionist discourse, gnostic-manipulationist topics and emphases evoke a desire to become one of the "elect" who understand the "hidden, secret mystery" and are gathered by the Son of man into eternal life.

In Mark 15–16, thaumaturgical discourse is present in references to darkness covering the whole land at the hour of Jesus' death (15:33–37), the curtain of the temple splitting from top to bottom (15:38), the stone that has mysteriously rolled back from the door of Jesus' tomb (16:4), and Jesus' rising up from death and exit from the tomb (16:6). The discourse introduces the possibility of a thaumaturgical response by God upon Jesus during the crucifixion (15:30, 32), only to delay it until the context of his death and burial in a tomb.

Revolutionist statements in other parts of the narrative establish a context in which Jesus' death and resurrection in Mark 15–16 are part of God's destruction of the powers of the created order and creation of a new order. Only the coming of the Son of man in the future, however, will be the time when the revolution fully occurs. The span of time between the death of Jesus and the coming of the Son of man creates temporal space for less dominant modes of discourse in the narrative to guide people's lives. It should not be surprising that the scribe who composed the longer ending of Mark allowed thaumaturgical discourse to dominate in it (16:9, 12, 14, 17–20). In the longer ending, emphasis on belief (16:11, 13, 14, 16–17) creates a space for emphasis on either a conversionist or a gnostic-manipulationist mode of life in the world until the return of the Son of man.

B. Common Social and Cultural Topics

Everyone living in an area knows common social and cultural topics either consciously or instinctively. Becoming an adult in that environment means acquiring knowledge, consciously or unconsciously, of these social and cultural values, patterns, or codes. Common social and cultural topics are the overall environment for the specific social topics in a text. Knowing the common social and cultural topics in a text can help an interpreter to avoid ethnocentric and anachronistic interpretation. The word "ethnocentrism" refers to basing interpretations on the values one's own people consider central to life. One of the goals of social-scientific critics during the last two decades has been to show that both North American and European interpretations of the Bible are based on individualist, guilt-oriented values rather than group-oriented, honor-shame values characteristic of Mediterranean society. The word "anachronism" refers here to presupposing something for one period of time that was present only during a different period of time. Another goal of social-scientific critics has been to distinguish between social systems in preindustrial, agrarian-based society and our postindustrial, urban-centered society. Anachronistic interpretations unconsciously impose our social-economic systems of production and distribution on meanings and values in first-century Mediterranean society that were the context for the production of the New Testament texts. The following topics represent social and cultural arenas in which distinctions need to be drawn between dominant modes of behavior and understanding in North American and European society and dominant modes of behavior and understanding in first-century Mediterranean society. Although most of the following headings suggest areas of difference between these ancient and modern societies, discussion will be confined to the first-century society, the assumption being that readers already have a grasp of the twentieth-century components.

I. Honor, Guilt, and Rights Cultures

Viewed from a male perspective that dominates first-century Mediterranean discourse,[1] *honor* stands for a person's rightful place in society, one's social standing. This place of honor is marked off by boundaries of power, sexual status, and position on the social ladder. Honor is a claim to worth along with the social acknowledgment of worth. The purpose of honor is to serve as a social rating that entitles a person to interact in specific ways with his or her equals, superiors, and subordinates, according to the prescribed cultural cues of the society. *Ascribed honor* befalls or happens to a person passively through birth, family connections, or endowment by notable persons of power. *Acquired honor* is honor actively sought and garnered most often at the expense of one's equals in the social contest of challenge and response.

Honor has a male and a female component. From a male perspective, the *male aspect* is called honor, while the *female aspect* is called shame. *Shame* in this context refers to a person's sensitivity about what others think, say, and do with regard to his or her honor.

•

Males dominate the action in Mark 15. Thus, honor is at stake throughout the chapter. Pilate is concerned to maintain honor in a setting where members of the temple hierarchy bring Jesus to him bound as a criminal. The narrative does not tell the reader if Pilate has ascribed honor from birth or

---

1. Much of this section is taken verbatim from Malina 1993: 28–62; see Myers 1988: 198–200; Neyrey 1991: 26–65.

family. There is an assumption, however, that Pilate enjoys acquired honor among certain colleagues who have invested him with special power in Jerusalem. As the narrative recounts the story, Pilate's honor is at stake in the manner in which he deals with Jesus once the members of the temple hierarchy have delivered him bound as a criminal. Pilate maintains a certain kind of "social rating" with both the temple hierarchy and the crowd by flogging Jesus and delivering him to soldiers to crucify him. On the other hand, the story negotiates with the reader a certain kind of honor for Pilate when he finds no crime guilty of death within Jesus. In addition, the narrative portrays Pilate as an honorable man when he seeks eyewitness information and releases the corpse of Jesus to Joseph of Arimathea (Mark 15:43–45).

According to Bruce Malina and Richard Rohrbaugh, the choice of crucifixion as the mode for Jesus' death submits Jesus to the "ultimate in public degradation and humiliation" (1992: 276). They refer to the sequence of events as a "status degradation ritual," "a process of publicly recasting, relabeling, humiliating, and thus recategorizing a person as a social deviant" (1992: 273). In addition, they perceive the Roman soldiers' mockery of Jesus as "King of the Judeans" to bring insult and dishonor on the population of Jerusalem, which had called for his humiliation and death (1992: 275). In the end, Pilate allows Jesus to have an honorable burial. "Romans often denied burial to criminals.... This passage [15:42–47] underscores Jesus' honorable burial, in spite of the dishonorable manner of his death and the incidents that lead up to it" (1992: 276).

Mark 15 features women "watching from afar" as Joseph buries Jesus, and they come to the tomb after the sabbath to anoint his body (15:40–41; 16:1). According to a male-oriented first-century Mediterranean social system as current social-scientific critics reconstruct it, these women are enacting "shame" as a positive value. Shame in this context takes the positive form of "following and serving" Jesus from the time he was in Galilee until he came to Jerusalem. The women continue this role when they come to the tomb to "serve" his body after it is buried. From the perspective of current social-scientific reading of this account, then, these women enact the role of "shame" in exemplary manner (Malina 1993: 50–55).

2. Dyadic and Individualist Personalities

A *dyadic personality* is one who needs another person continually in order to know who he or she really is.[2] Such persons internalize and make their own what others say, do, and think about them, because they believe it is necessary, for being human, to live out the expectations of others. These persons

---

2. Much of this section is taken verbatim from Malina 1993: 63–89; see Myers 1988: 46; Neyrey 1991: 67–96.

conceive of themselves as always interrelated to other persons while occupying a distinct social position both horizontally (with others sharing the same status, moving from center to periphery) and vertically (with others above and below in social rank). Such persons need to test this interrelatedness, with the focus of attention away from ego, on the demands and expectations of others who can grant or withhold reputation. In other words, dyadic personalities are people whose self-perception and self-image are formed in terms of what others perceive and feed back to them.

Modern individualism leads us to perceive ourselves as unique because we are set apart from other unique and set-apart beings. In contrast, a first-century person perceived himself or herself as a distinctive whole *set in relation* to other such wholes and *set within* a given social and natural background. Every individual was perceived as embedded in other individuals, in a sequence of embeddedness.

•

Mark 15 features Pilate as a dyadic personality checking out his own status both with Jesus and with the crowd in Jerusalem. Pilate is filled with wonderment (probably "confusion" or "frustration") when Jesus does not speak to him (15:5). As a dyadic personality, he wants "feedback" from Jesus as a medium for negotiating his honor status with himself. Pilate seeks and receives feedback from the crowd, which leads him to flog Jesus and send him off to be crucified. In Pilate's position of power, only a strong "individualist" could have made a decision to release Jesus without punishment. Throughout the chapter, then, the narrative depicts Pilate fulfilling the role of a dyadic personality in a stereotypical manner.

In contrast to Pilate, Jesus' dyadic relationship exists with God rather than humans. Jesus does not seek feedback on his identity and status from other people in the setting. Rather, his interaction is directly with God. He prays to God in Gethsemane (14:36) and cries out to God at his death (15:34). A distinctive aspect of Jesus' activity during the passion, then, is its embeddedness in a dyadic relation to God rather than to any humans — whether they be his disciples, the crowds of people, Pharisees and scribes, temple leaders, Pilate, soldiers, or centurions. In a previous context, I have emphasized the manner in which Jesus enacts his role without continual conversation with God (1992a: 116–19), and Wayne Merritt has discussed the "autonomy" of Jesus and of Paul in the New Testament (1993: 153–65). From the perspective of social-scientific theory about the first-century world of the Gospels, autonomy on behalf of Jesus would be a matter of internalizing a dyadic relation to God rather than establishing an "individualist" personality free from concern about the opinions of others. For Jesus, the primary "other" would be his "father God."

3. Dyadic and Legal Contracts and Agreements

A *dyadic contract* is an implicit agreement informally binding pairs of contractants rather than groups.[3] It is based on the informal principle of reciprocity, which is the most significant form of social interaction in the limited-good world (see section 7 below) of the first century. Reciprocity is an implicit, nonlegal contractual obligation, unenforceable by any authority apart from one's sense of honor and shame. By means of this principle of reciprocity, the honorable man selects (or is selected by) another for a series of ongoing, unspecified acts of mutual support.

In a limited-good world, such contracts can bind persons of equal status (colleague contracts) or persons of different statuses (patron-client contracts). The informal contracts function side by side with the formal contracts of society like buying and selling, marriage, and the natural covenant with God. The dyadic contract crosscuts the formal contracts of the culture, serving as the glue that holds individuals together for long or short terms and enabling the social interdependence necessary for life.

Both colleague contracts and patron-client contracts are initiated by means of positive challenges.

A *colleague contract* is a type of reciprocity among equals. It is symmetrical reciprocity between closely located persons of the same social status. The positive challenge initiating a colleague contract may be giving an invitation to supper, giving a small gift, or a benefaction like healing. These signal the start of an ongoing reciprocal relationship. Within a closed system, there are no free gifts. Each invitation is a positive challenge, a gift that requires repayment. Such positive challenges and appropriate responses will continue indefinitely, embracing a range of goods and services, provided that an exactly even balance between two partners is never struck.

A *patron-client contract* is initiated by means of a positive challenge, a positive gift. It ties persons of significantly different social statuses; hence the goods and services in the ongoing reciprocal relationship are different. The relationship is asymmetrical since the partners are not social equals and make no pretense to equality. The patron-client contract provides things not normally available in the village or urban neighborhood, things that at times are badly needed.

Patron-client relationships seem to be implied in the Gospels when people approach Jesus for "mercy." Furthermore, all positive relationships with God are rooted in the perception of patron-client contracts.

•

The major patron-client relations enacted in Mark 15 appear to be between Pilate and various people. Pilate treats the soldiers under him as clients who

---

3. Much of this section is taken verbatim from Malina 1993: 99–103; see Potter, Diaz, and Foster 1967.

are obligated to reciprocate for benefits they receive from him as long as they are under his charge. The soldiers take special benefits for themselves as clients of Pilate, to which they are probably entitled, when they divide Jesus' clothes among themselves (15:24). Joseph of Arimathea approaches Pilate as a client when he requests the corpse of Jesus from him. Pilate proves to be an honorable patron of those who honor Jesus when he allows Joseph to give Jesus an honorable burial.

Perhaps a patron-client relation is present between God and Jesus in Mark 15–16. In Mark 14:36, Jesus addresses God as "Abba, father," and requests that the ordeal of the crucifixion be removed. Nevertheless, Jesus accepts the will of God, the patron benefactor of all, including Jesus. In return for Jesus' willingness to die a humiliating death on the cross, God transforms Jesus' corpse into a body that can rise up from death and be absent from the tomb.

4. Challenge-Response (Riposte)

Challenge-response (*riposte*) is a sort of constant tug of war, a game of push and shove.[4] It is a type of social communication in which messages are transferred from a source to a receiver. The source here is the challenger, while the message is a symboled thing (a word, a gift, an invitation) or event (some action) or both. The channels are always public, and the *publicity* of the message guarantees that the receiving individual will react in some way, since even his nonaction is publicly interpreted as a response.

Challenge-response within the context of honor has at least three phases: (*a*) the challenge in terms of some action (word, deed, or both) on the part of the challenger; (*b*) the perception of the message by both the individual to whom it is directed and the public at large; and (*c*) the reaction of the receiving individual and the evaluation of the reaction on the part of the public.

The *challenge* is a claim to enter the social space of another. This claim may be positive or negative. A positive reason for entering the social space of another would be to gain some share in that space or to gain a cooperative, mutually beneficial foothold. A negative reason would be to dislodge another from his social space, either temporarily or permanently. Thus the source sending the message — always interpreted as a challenge — puts out some behavior, either positive (like a word of praise, a gift, a sincere request for help, a promise of help plus the actual help) or negative (a word of insult, a physical affront of various degrees, a threat along with the attempt to fulfill it). All such actions constitute the message that has to be perceived and interpreted by the receiving individual as well as the public at large.

---

4. Much of this section is taken verbatim from Malina 1993: 42–45; see Neyrey 1991: 28–32, 36–38, 49–52.

The *receiver* looks upon the action from the viewpoint of its potential to dishonor his self-esteem, his self-worth. He has to judge whether and how the challenge falls within the socially acknowledged range of such actions, from a simple questioning of self-esteem to an outright attack on self-esteem to a total denial of self-esteem. *Perception of the message* is a sort of second step.

The interaction over honor, the challenge-response game, is meant to take place only among equals. The receiver must judge whether he is equal to the challenger, whether the challenger honors him by regarding him as an equal, as is implicit in the challenge, or whether the challenger dishonors him by implying equality when there is none, either because the receiver is of a higher level or a lower level.

The third step in the interaction is the *reaction to the message,* involving the receiver's behavior that enables the public to pass a verdict: a grant of honor taken from the receiver of a challenge and awarded to the successful challenger or a loss of honor by the challenger in favor of the successful recipient of the challenge.

The challenge, then, is a threat to usurp the reputation of another, to deprive another of his reputation. When the person challenged cannot or does not respond to the challenge posed by his equal, he loses his reputation in the eyes of the public. People will say he cannot or does not know how to defend his honor. He thus loses his honor to the challenger, who correspondingly gains in honor. This set of cultural cues of perception, action, and belief is symboled in the behavior of conquering kings who take on the titles of the ones they vanquish. It is likewise symboled in the behavior of early Christians, who applied to the resurrected Jesus all the titles of those who were to overcome evil and death: Messiah, Lord, son of David, and son of God.

In the first-century Mediterranean world, every social interaction that took place outside one's family or outside one's circle of friends was perceived as a challenge to honor, a mutual attempt to acquire honor from one's social equal. Because of this constant and steady cue in Mediterranean culture, anthropologists call it an *agonistic culture.* The word *agon* is Greek for an athletic context or a contest between equals of any sort. Thus gift-giving, invitations to dinner, debates over issues of law, buying and selling, arranging marriages, arranging what we might call cooperative ventures for farming, business, fishing, mutual help, and the like — all these sorts of interaction take place according to the patterns of honor called challenge-response. Even honor and reputation, like all goods in life, are limited. Therefore, every social interaction comes to be perceived as an affair of honor, a contest or game of honor, in which players are faced with wins, ties, and losses.

•

There is a series of challenge-responses in Mark 15. The united action of the temple hierarchy in handing Jesus over to Pilate is a challenge by the temple leaders to Pilate as the prefect of Jerusalem. Pilate must respond to their challenge in an appropriate manner or he will put the public status of his position in jeopardy. The challenge consists of "entering the space" of Pilate and delivering Jesus to him. Pilate's initial response to the challenge is to interrogate Jesus (15:3).

Before the challenge by the temple leaders reaches any definitive conclusion, the narrative depicts "the crowd" presenting a second challenge to Pilate in the context of narration that informs the reader that it was the custom for Pilate to release a prisoner of their choice during the festival. Pilate responds by asking the crowd to choose between Jesus and Barabbas, whom the narrative describes as a murderous insurrectionist (15:7). Pilate embodies honor when he retorts with a question concerning what evil Jesus has done (15:14). Markan narration makes the resistance of Pilate extremely brief, however. In contrast to the narration in Luke (23:4), Pilate never asserts that he finds no guilt in Jesus. Markan narration simply asserts that Pilate perceived that the chief priests delivered Jesus to him out of envy (Mark 15:10). It also depicts action of the chief priests to be the cause of the request by the crowd for Pilate to crucify Jesus (15:11). In the end, Pilate responds to the challenges by the temple leaders and the crowd by "pleasing the crowd" through the action of flogging Jesus and delivering him to be crucified (15:15).

In the context of the challenges and responses to Pilate by the chief priests and the crowd, Mark 15 presents two challenges to Jesus. The first comes from Pilate when he asks Jesus if he is King of the Jews. Jesus' response, "You say so" (15:2), may seem clever or appropriate to the modern reader, but in the terms of the Mediterranean challenge-response system, this response does not establish or maintain Jesus' honor in the eyes of Pilate. The same is true of his silence in response to the accusations of the chief priests and the people. This silence leaves Pilate in wonderment. Although the nature of Pilate's wonder is not clear, it is certain that neither Jesus' words nor his silence was "honorable." At the end of the interaction, Pilate initiates actions that reveal the extent to which, within this cultural system, Jesus has been dishonored: crucifixion is among the most dishonorable deaths imaginable.

The second challenge to Jesus' honor comes while he hangs on the cross, as people who pass by, chief priests and scribes, issue the mocking challenge that he should come down from the cross (15:30, 32). Again, Jesus is silent in the face of these remarks, a silence that itself communicates how deeply dishonored he is within the Mediterranean system. The failure to respond to such a challenge dishonors him. For the reader who accepts the narrational perspective that Jesus is the Messiah, the challenges are of course ironic. The irony is that, while Jesus is thoroughly dishonored within the challenge-response paradigm of Mediterranean culture, his silent acceptance of his humiliating death demonstrates his obedience to the will of God. For the narrator and the reader who accepts the narrational point of view, the very silence that apparently dishonors Jesus is the source of his greatest honor.

5. Agriculturally Based, Industrial, and Technological Economic Exchange Systems

We live in a postindustrial, urban-centered society.[5] This is very different from the agrarian-based exchange systems of first-century Mediterranean society that are the context for the statements and interactions in New Testament literature. Social-scientific critics describe the distribution systems in preindustrial, agrarian-based society in the following ways.

Reciprocity was a clan-based system. Among members of a family, goods and services were freely given (*full reciprocity*). Among members of a cadet line within a clan, gifts were given; but an eye was kept on the balanced return-flow of countergifts (*weak reciprocity*). Where distant tribal kin were involved, the element of watchful calculation grew greater, and the time within which the countergift would have to be made grew less (*balanced reciprocity*). Outside the tribe mutuality ends — like morality, it holds good only for tribesmen. An outsider was fair game for clever dealing in an exchange: one could haggle, cheat, and lie (*negative reciprocity*).

Redistribution marked the historical transition from tribalism to more stable and centralized communities, usually organized around a shrine or temple.

The earliest civilizations of Mediterranean antiquity, those of Mesopotamia and Egypt, were based on a very distinctive mode of exchange, the *central storehouse economy*. This appears to have originated in Sumer and spread to Egypt. Initially a *priestly group* mobilized its labor force, the slaves of the god, to labor on the temple lands. The temple acted as central storehouse. Produce was stockpiled within that storehouse and redistributed to feed the temple's nonagricultural workforce (generally artisans and female weavers) as well as the agriculturists who produced it. In the off-season the workforce was turned to ditching, diking, and temple building. The priests held authority over their communities. They alone exercised control and direction. All others obeyed. Thus was born internal peace and order, and with it, the state.

•

Mark 15 exhibits interaction over a huge land mass between the leaders of a temple economy and the official representative of an emperor who maintained his position of power through a complex military institution throughout the Mediterranean world. The accusation the Roman prefect Pilate understands the priests to be making is that Jesus claims or aspires to be king over them (15:2, 9, 12). Since the traditional role of kings was to establish power over priests and their central storehouse economies, the "envy" the narrative imputes to the chief priests through Pilate's perceptions (15:10) would play into conventional understanding of the rivalry between priests and kings in the Mediterranean world.

---

5. Much of this section is taken verbatim from Malina 1993: 90–116; see Carney 1975: 167–74; Myers 1988: 48–54; Neyrey 1991: 125–79.

6. Peasants, Laborers, Craftspeople, and Entrepreneurs

Peasants came into existence after the growth of the preindustrial city.[6] They were rural smallholders under the control of outsiders. They had to exchange part of what they produced for manufactured goods that they could not make themselves, in some form of instrumental exchange in which they played only a subordinate role.

The peasant operated in terms of the family labor year. First, he and his family had to grow enough food to keep him and them and their livestock until the next harvest, with enough seed-grain to plant next year's crop. Second, the peasant had to produce a surplus: enough to obtain the occasional iron implement or utensil, to contribute to local festivals, and to make a loan to a neighbor in need. Only by contributing to festivals and making such loans was he able to acquire the reciprocal right to call on his neighbor when he himself was in adversity. From such festivals stemmed the little traditions of peasantry — peasant social insurance. Third, and (from the peasant's viewpoint) last, the peasant had to produce "funds of rent" adequate to satisfy his landlord or tax collector, the feared representative of the high culture or "Great Tradition" (see Wolf 1966: chap. 1).

•

The clearest representative of peasant people in Mark 15 appears to be Simon the Cyrene. "Coming from the field," he is compelled by the soldiers to carry Jesus' cross for him (15:21).

7. Limited, Insufficient, and Overabundant Goods

To make ends meet — supply his household, meet his local group obligations, and pay his funds of rent — the peasant had to keep his desires and living standards to an absolute minimum.[7] Hence the peasant developed a stance of "wantlessness." Peasants did not have a desire for ever more and more goods. Rather, they perceived that all goods are limited. This was the peasant idea of the *limited good*. The idea was that all good things — food, land, honor, standing — were in fixed quantities and short supply. Because their quantities could not be increased, if one peasant gained a greater share of any one of them than heretofore, he was thought to have done so at the cost of all his fellows. This notion was the cause of unending, unrelenting struggle and suspicion in peasant communities. The only viable strategy, as a result, was wantlessness. Few would push themselves forward as leaders. If an unusually large surplus was somehow produced, it was spent on a festival, to

---

6. Much of this section is taken verbatim from Malina 1993: 90–116; see Wolf 1966; Carney 1975: 198–99; Myers 1988: 51; Neyrey 1991: 154–60.

7. Much of this section is taken verbatim from Malina 1993: 90–116; see Carney 1975: 198–99; Myers 1988: 52.

propitiate the group. These ideas and practices put the peasantry, leaderless and resourceless, at the mercy of outsiders.

•

Mark 15 features two *lêstai*, social bandits (Malina and Rohrbaugh 1992: 270–71, 275) crucified alongside Jesus. These bandits, in addition to the murderous revolutionist Barabbas, represent the continuous struggle between the centralized temple economy, with its cooperative contracts with the Roman prefect, and peasant communities that were forced to support the position of authority, privilege, and luxury of the temple economy.

8. Purity Codes

Purity is about the general cultural map of social time and space, about arrangements with the space thus defined, and especially about the boundaries separating the inside from the outside.[8] The unclean or impure does not fit the space in which it is found, belongs elsewhere, and causes confusion in the arrangement of the generally accepted social map because it overruns boundaries.

At the time of Jesus, classification of the population in terms of degrees of purity derived from proximity to the Jerusalem temple with its large area of courts and buildings, the central, pivotal locus being the sanctuary, the holy of holies (Malina 1993: 159–60). The classification was as follows:

1. Priests

2. Levites

3. Full-blooded Israelites ("laymen")

4–6. Illegal children of priests
Proselytes or Gentile converts to Judaism
Proselytes who once were slaves: proselyte freedmen

7–10. Bastards (born of incestuous or adulterous unions)
"Fatherless" (born of prostitutes)
Foundlings
Eunuchs made so by men

11–13. Eunuchs born that way
Those with deformed sexual features
Hermaphrodites

14. Gentiles, that is, non-Jews

---

8. Much of this section is taken verbatim from Malina 1993: 149–83; see Myers 1988: 71, 75–77, and passim; Douglas 1966, 1972.

The Markan narrative attributes the crucifixion of Jesus to priests who capture him, turn him over to Pilate, and stir up the crowd to insist that Pilate crucify him. This means that the people at the top of the temple purity system commit themselves to the destruction of a Galilean whom they perceive to be a troublemaker. After Jesus dies on the cross, a member at the bottom of the list, a Gentile centurion, asserts that Jesus was a son of God (15:39). Mark 15, then, appears to enact an inversion of the purity system presupposed by the temple hierarchy. Priests at the top of the system enact a negative identity, while a Gentile at the bottom of the system makes an honorable statement about Jesus in the context of his death.

C. Final Cultural Categories

Aristotle describes, in his *Art of Rhetoric,* final cultural categories of rhetoric as "final topics" — those topics that most decisively identify one's cultural location. Cultural location, in contrast to social location, concerns the manner in which people present their propositions, reasons, and arguments both to themselves and to other people. These topics separate people in terms of dominant culture, subculture, counterculture, contraculture, and liminal culture. Again, as an interpreter approaches New Testament literature, cultural topics appear in the form of different kinds of culture rhetoric. The recent study of sociology of culture provides our insight on the different kinds of culture, and our analysis brings this information to New Testament interpretation in terms of different kinds of culture rhetoric (Robbins 1993b).

1. *Dominant culture rhetoric* presents a system of attitudes, values, dispositions, and norms that the speaker either presupposes or asserts are supported by social structures vested with power to impose its goals on people in a significantly broad territorial region.

2. *Subculture rhetoric* imitates the attitudes, values, dispositions, and norms of dominant culture rhetoric, and it claims to enact them better than members of dominant status. This rhetoric implies that a network of groups and institutions exists for supporting persons throughout their entire life cycle. Both sexes, all ages, and complete family groups are perceived to have a stake in this rhetoric (Roberts 1978: 112; Gordon 1970: 155).

Ethnic subculture rhetoric is a particular kind of subculture rhetoric. It has origins in a language different from the languages in the dominant culture, and it attempts to preserve and perpetuate an "old system" in a dominant cultural system in which it now exists, either because a significant number of people from this ethnic culture have moved into a new cultural environment or because a new cultural system is now imposing itself on it. A particular strategy of ethnic rhetoric appears to be a focused attack on only a few elements of the larger society, rather than on that society as a whole. This helps the ethnic subculture establish and maintain boundaries by which it may be identified (Barth 1969, 1981; Østergård 1992; Goudriaan 1992).

3. *Counterculture or alternative culture rhetoric* rejects *explicit* and *mutable* characteristics of the dominant or subculture rhetoric to which it responds (Roberts 1978: 114). The term is best reserved for intracultural phenomena; counterculture rhetoric is a culturally heretical rhetoric that evokes "a new future," not an alien rhetoric that evokes the preservation of an "old culture (real or imagined)" (Roberts 1978: 121). Counterculture rhetoric implies "alternative minicultures which make provisions for both sexes and a wide range of age groups, which are capable of influencing people over their entire life span, and which develop appropriate institutions to sustain the group in relative self-sufficiency" (at least twenty-five years) (Roberts 1978: 113). Counterculture rhetoric evokes the creation of "a better society, but not by legislative reform or by violent opposition to the dominant culture." The theory of reform manifest in its rhetoric provides an alternative and hopes "that the dominant society will 'see the light' and adopt a more 'humanistic' way of life." In other words, "social reform is not a preoccupation" of counterculture rhetoric (Roberts 1978: 121). It evokes a willingness to live one's own life and let the members of dominant society go on with their "madness." Yet an underlying theme is the *hope* of voluntary reform by the dominant society in accord with a different model of "the good life." Hence, one would expect fully developed counterculture rhetoric to express a *constructive* image of an alternative, better way of life. It provides a relatively self-sufficient system of action by grounding its views in a well-developed, supporting ideology (Roberts 1978: 121).

4. *Contraculture or oppositional culture rhetoric* is a "short-lived, counter-dependent cultural deviance" of dominant culture, subculture, or counterculture rhetoric (Roberts 1978: 124). It is "groupculture" rhetoric rather than subculture or counterculture rhetoric. Contraculture rhetoric implies groups "that do not involve more than one generation, which do not elaborate a set of institutions that allow the group to be relatively autonomous and self-sufficient, and which do not sustain an individual over an entire life span" (Roberts 1978: 113). Contraculture rhetoric is primarily a reaction-formation response to some form of dominant culture, subculture, or counterculture rhetoric. This means that it does not create an alternative response on the basis of values it develops out of a different system of understanding, but it simply reacts in a negative way to certain values and practices in another culture. It often is possible, therefore, to predict the behavior and values evoked by contraculture rhetoric, since it simply inverts certain well-known behaviors and values in that other culture (Roberts 1978: 123–24; Yinger 1960: 629; Stark 1967: 141, 153; Ellens 1971: 91–107). Contraculture rhetoric, then, asserts "more negative than positive ideas" (Roberts 1978: 124, citing Bouvard 1975: 119). The positive ideas are simply presupposed and come from the culture to which it is reacting.

5. *Liminal culture rhetoric* is at the outer edge of identity (Bhabha 1992: 444). It exists only in the language it has for the moment. In some instances, liminal culture will appear as people or groups experience transition from one cultural identity to another. In other instances, liminal culture exists among individuals and groups that have never been able to establish a clear social and cultural identity in their setting. The language of a liminal culture is characterized by a "dialectic of culture and identification" that has neither binary nor hierarchical clarity. Its speech is disjunctive and multiaccentual (Bhabha 1992: 445). It starts and stops without obvious consistency or coherence. It features "minimal rationality" as a dialogic process that "attempts to track displacements and realignments that are the effects of cultural antagonisms and articulations — subverting the rationale of the hegemonic moment and relocating alternative, hybrid sites of cultural negotiation" (Bhabha 1992: 443).

•

In Mark 15, the Roman prefect Pilate functions in a dominant cultural mode, and priests, scribes, and elders function in a subcultural mode. The clash over Jesus' identity places him in a liminal cultural position. If the reader has thought that Jesus' action and speech represent a clear cultural alternative in the Mediterranean world, Mark 15 calls this into question. In a context where one of Jesus' male associates has betrayed him and the rest of his associates have fled, people mock Jesus' identity and role. Who is he? Is he King of the Jews? Is he the Messiah of Israel? If so, how can he be hanging on a tree in disgrace? Even the bandit-revolutionaries who hang on the cross beside him "revile" him (15:32). No clear cultural identity emerges for Jesus as he suffers and dies. In these scenes Jesus is neither a clear countercultural figure nor a clear contracultural figure. He is a liminal cultural figure — outside of Jewish culture and outside of Greco-Roman culture.

From the language of Roman officials, Pilate and a centurion, Jesus' identity is unclear. Is Jesus "King of Jews"? In what ways is he "son of God"? Jesus' identity is "up for grabs" and even laughable — mocked at by temple hierarchy, passersby, and bandit-criminals hanging on the cross beside him. Jesus cries out in a context of alienation from all people, and even from God. The mockery of people who pretend he is calling out to Elijah and the splitting of the temple curtain from top to bottom make statements that are confusing and unclear. Would anyone think Jesus were the Messiah if Elijah rescued him from the cross? What exactly does the splitting of the temple curtain mean? Jesus' identity is not clearly that of a king, a revolutionary, a prophet, or a philosopher dying for a particular cause. The language around him is "disjunctive" and "multiaccentual" (Bhabha 1992: 445). Often a definitive closure clarifies an identity, as there is in the account of the death of Eleazar in 4 Maccabees or of Akiba in the Talmud. But not in the Markan account. Interpreters have not been able to agree whether Jesus' death cry is a cry of confidence or alienation. They cannot agree if the centurion is responding to Jesus' death or to the splitting of the temple curtain. The discourse cannot agree if the centurion is referring to Jesus as "the" son of God or "a" son of God. The discourse is culturally liminal — partly Jewish and partly Greco-Roman, but not totally Jewish or totally Greco-Roman. The alternative, of course, would be for the discourse to evoke a fully Christian cultural discourse, but that is not the case either. Jesus does not die as a full embodiment of "very God of very God" and "very man of very man." He dies like a human being forced by God to accept death against his own will (Mark 14:36), not like a divine being in charge of his own destiny. The Gospel of John changes this as Jesus identifies the hour in which he himself is glorified and in which "God is glorified in him" (John 13:31). In Mark, the discourse is liminal Christian discourse as well as liminal Jewish and Greco-Roman discourse. Who is Jesus? A Son of man who dies and will arise and return as Son of man. But his closest disciples dispute what this means, and even women who have attended to his needs from Galilee to Jerusalem flee in fright from his empty tomb. If they see Jesus again, they will see him at the outer limits of society and culture.

STUDY GUIDE:
Common Social and Cultural Topics —
The Woman Who Anointed Jesus

This is a study of the "social and cultural" intertexture of a story in the New Testament. Becoming familiar with social and cultural meanings is an important step in interpreting the text in the context of first-century Mediterranean society and culture. The early Christians lived in a world that is foreign to us. Access to food, housing, and health was governed by preindustrial modes of production and distribution rather than the modern technological conveniences and benefits we know today. Dominant military and political forces decided when they would move into a region and live off of its produce and taxes. Kinship relations — strong extended family ties — represented the basic networks that provided the basic needs of life, the power structures, and the conditions for protection or destruction.

Honor and shame were dominant cultural values that governed people's lives as a result of everyone's substantial dependence on traditional loyalties and relationships. Clear rules of hospitality accompanied the honorable person, and strict rules of appropriate exchange (reciprocity) were operative at all levels of society. People presupposed that all goods (including honor) were in limited supply; thus extravagance on anyone's behalf always created a scarcity for someone else.

Honor was given and taken through public encounters. This created an "agonistic" culture, one in which equals regularly were engaged in contests or games of honor that held the prospect of a win, a tie, or a loss (see Malina 1993: 28–62). Social theorists refer to such an encounter as "challenge-response (*riposte*)." A challenger communicates some kind of message in public, and the public nature of the act guarantees that the receiving individual will react (see Malina 1993: 34–44). The Gospels and Letters in the New Testament exhibit a vigorous environment of exchanges of honor and shame as a context in which Christian belief was defined, maintained, and extended to new individuals and groups.

•

1. Read the story of the woman who anointed Jesus in Luke 7:36–50. Who offers hospitality to whom at the beginning of the story (7:36)? What presuppositions about economic status and social prestige do you think underlie the ability to offer this kind of hospitality? The Greek words translated "took his place at the table" mean "reclined at table," which indicates that the Pharisee was hosting a significant meal, a "luxury meal," for his guests. For this depiction of the status of Pharisees (remember that this account was being written ca. 80–90 C.E.) in the Gospel of Luke, compare Luke 11:37; 14:1; 16:10–14. Also notice how the Pharisees befriend Jesus in Luke 13:31–32.

2. What kinds of social issues do you think accompany the actions of the woman in 7:37–39? Would her actions ordinarily be appropriate in this setting? Is there anything unusual about her actions? Do you think it would be appropriate for a woman to be present in this part of the house during this meal? What kind of women, if any, could appropriately be present in the part of the house where this kind of meal was being offered? Some social theorists refer to "shame" as a "positive role that women played (and which many still play today)" in Mediterranean society and elsewhere. How do you think "shame" could and can function as a "positive role" in traditional society?

3. The meanings in Luke 7:40–43 would be governed by patron-client relationships during the time of early Christianity. See the discussion of dyadic contracts above (pp. 79–79) and explain the use of the word "love" in 7:42 (also see Malina 1993: 99–103). Has the "patron" acted beyond the usual expectations of the contract? With this action, what kind of role has the "patron" taken? What kind of "relation" has the patron established with the debtor?

4. The meanings in Luke 7:44–46 would have been governed by laws of hospitality (see Pitt-Rivers 1968) and by honor-shame rituals. If Jesus is perceived to have social prestige, will it bring honor to the Pharisee to have Jesus as a guest? Why? While a person is a guest, that person is expected to show special honor to the host. Likewise, a host is expected to show special honor to a prestigious guest. What does Jesus claim about Simon the Pharisee and the appropriate hospitality rituals when he arrives?

5. In social terms, Jesus establishes a patron-client relation with the

woman on the basis of an exchange of "religious goods" in 7:47–48. Can you explain this and describe what it will mean for the woman in the future?

6. What kind of social and economic conditions do you think exist in the context where a Christian writer has written this story in this way? Do you think the writer envisions a location in a large city in the Mediterranean world, or is he thinking of social dynamics in a small village or town? Does Simon the Pharisee seem to be a person "sent out" by leaders of the Jerusalem temple, or does he seem to have a social and economic base independent from the temple and its leaders? Do you think the author of Luke is thinking of Pharisees in the village-town environment of Galilee during the first part of the century, or do you think he is thinking of Pharisees in a large city in Asia Minor, Greece, or Rome as he writes this version of the story?

STUDY GUIDE:
Social and Cultural Texture — John 9

The world of the Gospel of John (commonly called the Fourth Gospel) is intricate, harmonic, melodic, textured, episodic, colorful, and dramatic. Even more, the Johannine world is comprehensive, is totalistic, and offers a variegated schema for understanding the universe. In order to communicate this world, the stories and sayings are developed into more complex scenes than in many other books in the Bible. Sayings are developed into discourses, and healing stories and sayings are developed into dramatic scenes that cover a complete chapter. If we want to know the Johannine world, we will follow through the harmonic developments and watch the ideas volley back and forth across the Johannine world until the final episode is over. Once the author introduces a story or a saying, he will often refuse to let it go until he has developed features of that story or saying into a harmonic display of the Johannine world.

This study uses the drama of the healing of the blind man to explore the *social and cultural texture* of narrative and speech in the Gospel of John. Here there are three major areas of social and cultural texture. First, there are "specific social topics" in narrative and in attributed speech (conversionist, revolutionist, introversionist, gnostic-manipulationist, thaumaturgical, reformist, and/or utopian). Second, there are "common social and cultural topics" in narrative and in speech (issues like honor, patron-client contracts, challenge-response, reciprocity, limited good, and purity codes). Third, there are "final cultural topics" (dominant, subculture, counterculture, contraculture, or liminal culture rhetoric). This study guide pursues only the first and third major areas of social and cultural texture.

One of the ways to become aware of the distinctive features in the Gospel of John is to compare it with the other New Testament Gospels. Another way is to follow a theme through the entire Gospel of John. Still another way is to follow the unfolding drama of a particular section, like the healing of the blind man in John 9.

•

1. Read and compare Mark 8:22–26 with John 9:1–7. Do you think it is correct to say that the Markan account of the story contains specific social topics of thaumaturgical discourse? Do you think additional specific social topics also are present in the discourse of the Markan story (conversionist, revolutionist, introversionist, etc.)?

Thaumaturgical topics also are present in John 9:1–7, are they not? Do you think it is correct to say that the Johannine account of the story intro-duces, in addition, specific social topics of "knowing" (gnostic-manipulationist topics)? Make a list of topics a person is supposed to "know" by the end of verse 7. Do you see evidence of other specific social topics in John 9:1–7?

2. In Mark, the action moves quickly from the healing story to an en-tirely new scene. This is typical in the Synoptic Gospels. John, in contrast, elaborates the miracle healing until the end of chapter 9. J. L. Martyn has suggested that this elaboration can be seen as a drama with seven scenes (Martyn 1968), with verses 1–7 as scene 1. Scene 2, then, is composed of verses 8–12. As in any good drama, the scene changes, new characters appear, and we are given new information.

Regular thaumaturgical specific topics are faith, courage, amazement, what it is possible for God to do, and so on. Do you see any thaumaturgical specific topics in John 9:8–12?

Regular gnostic-manipulationist specific topics are knowing and questions like: Why are we all here on earth? How did we get here? How can we be saved? Who will come and save us? Where will the one who comes to save us come from? Search for gnostic-manipulationist specific topics in John 9:8–12. If you see any, make a list of them.

3. Scene 3 occurs in John 9:13–17. Who are the new major characters? Do these new characters ever question "the fact" that the blind man has been healed? If they do question this, they are pursuing thaumaturgical specific topics.

Do these new characters pursue gnostic-manipulationist specific topics? If they do, please describe them.

Do these new characters pursue other specific social topics (conversionist, revolutionist, etc.)? If so, describe them. If you do not find any others, you are not alone. But perhaps you do see some others.

The issue in scene 3 seems to center around the identity of the healer, Jesus ("who" he is). Who does the blind man believe Jesus to be? What about the other people? Is there agreement in the group?

Now let us move to final cultural categories in the scene. Does someone speak in the mode of dominant culture rhetoric in the scene?

Describe the cultural mode of "others" in the scene. Would you describe the mode of culture rhetoric in the speech of the "others" as subculture, counterculture, contraculture, or liminal culture rhetoric?

4. Scene 4 occurs in John 9:18–23. The narrator suddenly uses the term "the Jews" rather than the term "Pharisees." Essenes, followers of Jesus, followers of John the Baptist, Sadducees, Zealots, Pharisees, and "people of the land" could all be called "Jews" during this period of time. What would you say is the effect of shifting the narrational description of the speakers and actors from a specific group of Jews, namely, "Pharisees," to "the Jews"?

Who in John 9:18–23 speaks dominant culture rhetoric? What are the topics this mode of rhetoric addresses, and what is the nature of the rhetoric (theses [direct assertions], contraries, reasons, analogies, examples, citations of scripture)?

Do you see judicial rhetoric in the scene? Who is "holding a court trial" in the scene? Who are the interrogators, and what "witnesses" have been brought before the court?

What kind of culture rhetoric do the parents speak (dominant, sub-, counter-, contra-, or liminal)? On the basis of what words or modes of speech in the text would you describe their speech as a particular kind of rhetoric?

What cultural terminology would you use to describe the relation of the parents to "the Jews"? Do you think it was possible for followers of Jesus to maintain membership in synagogues at the time that John wrote? (Note: the verb "to put out" has the force of "to excommunicate" in the Greek.)

5. As in much drama, characters are brought together for a second confrontation in scene 5, John 9:24–34. Who are these characters, and what is the major issue? Of whom do the Pharisees say they are disciples?

Do you see a description of the formation of a counterculture in verse 28? Can you describe the dominant culture and the counterculture? Now look at verse 29. The Gospel of John features Jesus speaking counterculture rhetoric at this point in the story. Please look at John 5:46 and describe some of the content of the counterculture rhetoric as it develops its stance against the dominant culture the narration describes. What is the force of "and they drove him out" in verse 34? Remember what "to put out" meant in verse 22.

Are the specific social topics of verses 30–33 thaumaturgical, conversionist, gnostic-manipulationist, revolutionist, reformist, introversionist, or utopian? Do you see a combination of more than one of these kinds of specific social topics in these three verses?

6. John 9:35–41 is the final scene (one could divide it and name the inner scenes 6 and 7). In a dramatically symmetric way, Jesus reenters in this final scene, which balances his appearance in scene 1. What titles are used for Jesus? What does Jesus say that the blind man has done, which ultimately leads the blind man to say, "Lord, I believe"?

What is the nature of the specific social topics in this scene? Would you describe them as thaumaturgical, conversionist, gnostic-manipulationist, revolutionist, reformist, introversionist, or utopian? Do you see a combination of more than one type of specific social topic in the scene?

How does Jesus describe the Pharisees in verses 39 and 41? Glance over Matthew 23 for an interesting comparison. What is the cultural nature of the speech in the final scene? Do you think it would be accurate to say that the narrator presents Jesus as speaking strong counterculture rhetoric that changes the speech of the Pharisees from the form of dominant culture rhetoric (which they spoke at the beginning of the chapter) to liminal culture rhetoric that stands on the fringes of Johannine Christian counterculture? In other words, the speech of the Pharisees is characterized as no longer strong and decisive but as a kind of "confused static" from the point of view of the counterculture.

7. John is very interested in showing that "signs" have two levels of significance. The obvious meaning of John 9 is that Jesus was able to heal a man physically. What is the underlying or second level of meaning of John 9? The man was physically healed in scene 1. In what other way was the man healed, and in which scene? The emphasis on physical healing alone would evoke a thaumaturgical social location. What kind of social location does the second level of healing evoke?

Now think back to the account in Mark 8:22–26, where Jesus must act twice to complete the healing. Does this strange account have any more significance to you now?

Chapter 4

Ideological Texture

SHARING INTERESTS IN COMMENTARY AND TEXT

The primary subject of ideological analysis and interpretation is people. Texts are the secondary subject of ideological analysis, simply the object of people's writing and reading. The issue is the social, cultural, and individual location and perspective of writers and readers. Ideological analysis of a text, then, is simply an agreement by various people that they will dialogue and disagree with one another with a text as a guest in the conversation.

This means that analysis of the ideological texture of a text exists at the opposite end of the spectrum from analysis of the inner texture of a text. Inner texture concerns the words, phrases, and clauses of the text itself; ideological texture concerns the biases, opinions, preferences, and stereotypes of a particular writer and a particular reader. The beginning place for ideological analysis and interpretation, therefore, is analysis and interpretation of me, the writer of this sentence, and you, the reader of this sentence. The second place for ideological analysis and interpretation is other people's interpretation of a text in which we are interested. The third and last place for ideological analysis and interpretation is the text that is the guest in our interpretive conversation with each other.

Ideological analysis is more like intertextual analysis than inner textual analysis, since there are always two "texts" the interpreter is interactively analyzing. In intertextual analysis, an interpreter is analyzing both the text that is in the foreground of interest and one or more other texts. In ideological analysis, an interpreter is analyzing both himself or herself as a writer and reader and one or more other writers and readers.

A special characteristic of ideological analysis is its focus on the relation of individual people to groups. For interpreters of ideology, it is not very satisfactory to talk about "one person's ideology." One person's particular way of thinking is the subject of psychology and individual aesthetics rather than ideology. A person's ideology concerns her or his conscious or unconscious enactment of presuppositions, dispositions, and values held in common with other people.

As a result of their focus on commonly held values and points of view, ideological interpreters regularly use the concept of a "system" for their analyses. Thus, one definition of ideology is "an integrated system of beliefs, assumptions, and values" that reflects "the needs and interests of a group or class at a particular time in history" (Davis 1975: 14). John H. Elliott explains that "this integrated system proceeds from the need to understand, to interpret to self and others, to justify, and to control one's place in the world. Ideologies are shaped by specific views of reality shared by groups — specific perspectives on the world, society and man, and on the limitations and potentialities of human existence" (Elliott 1990: 268).

A. Individual Locations

The beginning place for ideological analysis and interpretation is with people, and the best place to begin is with you, the reader of this sentence. Only if you have significant insight into the ideological texture of your own presuppositions, dispositions, and values will you be able to analyze the ideological texture both of other people's interpretations of a text and of a text that is the mutual interest of you and another person who has interpreted it. The problem is that, in the dialogue between you and me here, I cannot analyze the ideological texture of your presuppositions, dispositions, and values; I can only analyze my own. Therefore, I will use myself as the subject for the analysis. If you accept the task of analyzing yourself in a similar manner, we can then move to other people besides you and me, and then we can finally move to the text that is the special guest in our interpretive conversation.

The first task is to reach back into the last chapter, on social and cultural texture, and analyze ourselves with the taxonomies in the sections entitled "Specific Social Topics" and "Final Cultural Categories."

First, where is your and my location in Bryan Wilson's spectrum of responses to the world, based on the specific social topics that dominate our discourse (see the section "Specific Social Topics" in chap. 3)? As a young person, I was primarily conversionist in orientation. Raised in an evangelical family that went to church every Sunday morning and most Sunday evenings, I thought that if the heart of every person in the world was changed, then the world would be changed into a place of salvation for all. What was your primary orientation when you were a young person? The other alternatives are revolutionist, introversionist, gnostic-manipulationist, thaumaturgical, reformist, or utopian.

As I have grown older, I have continued to value decisive changes both in myself and other people, but a reformist orientation has moved much more into the center of my discourse. I now believe that even the most well-meaning people do highly cruel things with the social, economic, and political powers available to them. For this reason, it is necessary to focus even more fully on the structures of interaction, distribution, and valuation in society than on the hearts of particular individuals. People with widely differing "hearts and minds" need to commit themselves to social, economic, and political structures that nurture, nourish, heal, and edify people of all classes, races, and social status. This means my primary orientation has become reformist rather than conversionist. What is your primary orientation now that you have become older? Has your primary orientation become different than it was when your parents or guardians were a dominant presence in your life?

In addition to my reformist orientation, which is primary, and my conversionist orientation, which is substantial, I am also significantly gnostic-manipulationist in orientation. In other words, primarily because of my father's energetic communication of his view of the world to me when I was a child, I possess a view of the world that is significantly different from the view I hear presented in the dominant culture of American society. My view is heavily influenced by a perception of personal, divine forces at work in the innermost nature of creation. To me the complexity of trees, animals, our bodies, rocks, and bugs brings wonderment about the life-nature of all being, including what we call inanimate, nonliving being. I know that, on the one hand, there are many people who share something of a similar view of the world. There are many, however, who do not. My sense is that the divine has revealed something of a view of the world that explains to me the innermost nature of my own being, the being of the world, and the meaning of death and life in the world. This means I also have a significant touch of gnostic-manipulationist response in my orientation to the world. What is your own special view of life and its meaning? Is there a third kind of response that is interrelated with other kinds in your response to the world?

Second, what is your and my cultural location, based on the spectrum of final cultural categories discussed in the last chapter? Again my location has changed as my life has progressed.

I was raised in a rural culture in Nebraska — literally in the middle of a section of land containing one-half mile dirt lanes from gravel roads to our house, near a village with a population of 139 people. We did not have electricity until I was in the second grade. Therefore, we did not have a pressurized water system or indoor plumbing. I rode a horse to school through the eighth grade. I became aware that I lived in a counterculture years before I went to high school. The other students listened regularly to radio programs during the time I was milking cows by hand and tending the other animals on the farm. Even after we had electricity, we did not have a television. The other students had knowledge about dominant American culture that I had no opportunity to experience. I was, however, a very good student. Math and spelling were always easy for me. I read books about horses, dogs, and the Bobbsey twins, and I heard a lot about the Bible when we went to church — though I never read extended portions of it. Repairing machinery, cars, and tractors was more natural to me than reading. I read books when I was being lazy. Most of the time I had to work. I liked being lazy and reading when I had time. But I also had to practice my piano lessons, which was another form of work. On Sunday afternoons, my brother and I went hunting for small animals we would shoot and clean for mom to cook. We enjoyed the special taste of rabbit, squirrel, pigeon, or pheasant. During my early years, therefore, I lived in a rural countercultural environment where work, going to school, and going to church were the three most important activities. What was the nature of the culture in which you were raised? The alternatives are dominant culture, subculture, counterculture, contraculture, or liminal culture.

Toward the end of high school, my family moved to Iowa, to a town of fifteen thousand people that was a twin city with a town of sixty thousand. We lived at the corner of Sixth and Main Streets in a small apartment. This was very different and significantly problematic for me. I did like the more leisurely life. The library was right across the street, and it was quite permissible for me to go there immediately after I came home from school! There were no cows to milk or animals to feed! I read books and tried to read newspapers, though I could not accurately remember the faces and names of all the people everyone else considered to be so important, and I could not clearly envision where all the countries were that the newspapers talked about. Soon I moved out and lived with a family that ran a dairy farm. I helped to milk cows morning and evening, and I did fieldwork with the tractors. Soon I was able to buy a car and go to college. I did well, returning home during the summers to work on the farm morning and evening and on construction in the city during the day. With this activity I paid my way through college. Then I got married and went to seminary in a major city in Ohio. This was my first extended experience of city life. The seminary was my primary culture there, and it was a good environment from which to begin to experience the cultural resources of urban culture in America.

After seminary, I moved to Hyde Park in Chicago with my wife and two children to attain a Ph.D. in biblical studies. This was an environment very different from the rural counterculture in which I was raised in Nebraska. I began to think seriously about my multicultural life. Still in many ways my heart was in rural, countercultural America. Yet I was a significant participant in educated urban culture, with its international and interracial population, networks, resources, values, and challenges. After this time, I lived sixteen years in a twin city area in Illinois with a population of one hundred thousand people and a university of thirty-five thousand people. For a year, my wife and I lived in a major city in Norway while I was a Fulbright Professor. Now my wife and I have lived more than a decade in Atlanta, Georgia — a growing, bustling city.

I have become more and more conscious of the multicultural nature of my existence, and this experience of multiple social and cultural locations has influenced the manner in which I interpret texts. Socio-rhetorical criticism is the embodiment of my multiple locations in society and culture.

•

What is the nature of your social and cultural location? Have you been mostly a participant in one culture during your lifetime? What is the nature of this culture? Are there multiple cultures and social locations that are still part of your life? If so, what are they, and how do you combine them in your interpretation of texts?

•

This social and cultural location gives me keen interest in Ched Myers's socially and culturally vibrant analysis of Mark 15 (Myers 1988: 369–97). His approach deeply attracts my interest because, whether right or wrong from the perspective of criteria in dominant Markan scholarship, it addresses issues that lie deeply in my body and soul as a result of my social and cultural location.

I am interested in what happens to village and town folk when they go into large cities. Myers probes Mark 15 from this perspective. Pilate has no interest in who Jesus really is and what he is about. He has an idea about "Jesus being a king," and he simply "confronts" Jesus with it (15:2). He "cannot understand how anyone can face the state's threat of capital punishment with such determination" (Myers 1988: 379). This is very characteristic of leaders located in cities. They are only interested in things that affect their power in their city and their "network" out to other cities. The scene that ensues with the crowd is a parody of gladiator games in the Coliseum at Rome where, after the fight, the crowd could choose "whether a wounded gladiator would be killed or allowed to live" (R. L. Merritt 1985: 68; Myers 1988: 381). Again, this is characteristic of the way in which "cities" deal with people from outside them. The police in Omaha looked with disdain on us and our truck when we took sheep to the stockyards. When a person ran his car up so close to our truck when we stopped at a stop sign on a hill that our truck rolled back and touched it as dad started out, the policeman had no interest at all in how natural it is for a truck to roll back about a foot when it is loaded heavily with animals who lurch and move as you start up. City people never think about such things. People drive their cars right up on your bumper and consider it your fault if you roll back even six inches. City police only follow "their rules" in their city. No one in Ithaca, Nebraska, would ever drive up that close behind a truck when it stops on a hill, I can tell you that. These things depend on your cultural and social location. Ched Myers does not hide these issues in his interpretation. He tries to deal with them, and I like that. The only problem is that now I live in a city, and have for many years. So I am implicated in this kind of "city view," probably, even when I am exhibiting aspects of life in the country. So I am some kind of mixture of rural and city being. Perhaps it is people who have somehow experienced a similar social and cultural "catchment" that feel some special kinship with the socio-rhetorical approach I have developed to interpret texts.

Myers notices, in addition, that only women "understand the true vocation of leadership" to which Jesus is committed. Women who have followed Jesus and "served" him "become the 'lifeline' of the discipleship narrative" (Myers 1988: 396). This is something I have experienced during my married life. If a person is fortunate, like I am, to have a wife who cares about his personal well-being, it is natural to respond positively to women's activities and leadership in New Testament texts. My social and cultural experiences in life, therefore, cause me to resonate deeply with Myers's commentary on Mark 15. Some of my colleagues may think I should leave these kinds of observations out of "scholarly" interpretation. It is necessary to be aware of them, however, or we get caught in a split between "mind" and "body" in analysis and interpretation of texts. Such a split actually makes our analyses less rigorous, precise, and scientific. Only if we have some ability to "see ourselves as others see us" will we be able to see Mark 15 as some other people may "naturally" see it.

B. Relation to Groups

Jeremy Boissevain has developed a taxonomy that Bruce Malina has introduced to New Testament interpreters for analysis of different kinds of groups. When considering one's ideology, an adapted form of this is a helpful guide alongside the taxonomies of Bryan Wilson and sociologists of culture. Boissevain's taxonomy, with some revisions, is as follows.

1. Clique

A clique is a coalition (a temporary alliance of distinct parties for a limited purpose [Boissevain 1974: 171]) whose members associate regularly with each other on the basis of affection and common interest and possess a marked sense of common identity (Boissevain 1974: 174). All members of a clique interact with one another. It is helpful to speak of *core members,* who participate all the time, *primary members,* who meet sometimes with the core and rarely alone, and *secondary members,* who are on the fringe and participate infrequently (Boissevain 1974: 179).

2. Gang

A gang is a leader-centered coalition (a temporary alliance of distinct parties for a limited purpose [Boissevain 1974: 171]) whose members associate regularly on the basis of affection and common interest and possess a marked sense of common identity. In short, a gang is a large clique with a single leader (Boissevain 1974: 181).

3. Action Set

An action set is a group of persons who join together as a coalition (a temporary alliance of distinct parties for a limited purpose [Boissevain 1974: 171]) to coordinate their actions to achieve a particular goal. Leadership emerges as or after they join forces to achieve the goal (Boissevain 1974: 186).

4. Faction

A faction is a coalition (a temporary alliance of distinct parties for a limited purpose [Boissevain 1974: 171]) of persons (followers) recruited personally according to structurally diverse principles by or on behalf of a person in conflict with another person or persons, with whom he or she was formerly united, over honor and/or control over resources. The central focus of the faction is the person who has recruited it, who may also be described as the leader (Boissevain 1974: 192).

Rivalry is basic to the existence of a faction, for a faction supports a person engaged in competition for honor or resources. The conflict is political. The prizes for which these persons compete may also include access to the "truth" (a form of power) and hence be ideological, as in a religious group or church. Factions compete with other coalitions for the same prizes. They are conflicting units formed within a larger encapsulating social entity such as a village, an association, or even another coalition that had previously been united. The longer the faction remains united, the more corporate characteristics it acquires (Boissevain 1974: 194–95).

5. Corporate Group

A corporate group is a body with a permanent existence: a collection of people recruited on recognized principles, with common interests and rules (norms) fixing rights and duties of the members in relation to one another and to these interests. The common interests can be called property interests if property is very broadly defined (Boissevain 1974: 171, quoting Mair 1965: 13).

6. Historic Tradition

A historic tradition is one to which a person exhibits special alliance when interpreting the Bible and the world. Examples are the Catholic tradition, the Protestant tradition, or a specific tradition (e.g., Lutheran or Reformed) within Protestantism.

7. Multiple Historic Traditions throughout the World

The phrase "multiple historic traditions throughout the world" refers to an approach that consciously relates New Testament interpretation not only to

Judaism, out of which Christianity emerged, but to traditions like Hinduism, Buddhism, Islam, and Native American religion.

The most obvious *corporate group* in North America related to biblical interpretation is the Society of Biblical Literature, founded in 1880. In 1988, a representative membership of this society authored a commentary on the Bible entitled *Harper's Bible Commentary*. The editorial committee selected John R. Donahue, S.J., to write the commentary on the Gospel of Mark (Donahue 1988), and his interpretation exhibits well the ideology of this corporate group of biblical scholars. One notices a strategy of balancing "credible scholarly alternatives" against one another, with a freedom by the author himself to state his own scholarly assessment of the issue. Views that have not been sanctioned by authoritative scholarly debate do not appear in the commentary.

Donahue recounts the early church tradition that identifies the author of the Second Gospel with John Mark, a companion of Peter, then asserts that this is "called into question by the apologetic desire to associate a non-apostolic Gospel with the apostle Peter, by the frequency of 'Mark' as a name in the Roman Empire, and by the ancient tendency to attribute works to important figures from the past." Patristic writers associated the final composition of the Gospel with Rome; some recent interpreters have located it in Galilee or southern Syria; and Donahue prefers to place its composition in the context of "a Jewish-Christian community at Rome shortly after A.D. 70" populated with people of "lower socioeconomic status" (Donahue 1988: 983–84). Donahue is concerned not to advance anti-Semitism with his interpretation. Jewish authorities may have interrogated Jesus, but the responsibility of a formal trial lies with the Romans. Pharisees do not participate in the final passion events in Mark, "so not all Jewish leaders, and certainly not the mass of Jewish people at the time of Jesus, rejected Jesus or were responsible for his death" (Donahue 1988: 1006). Jesus is abandoned by his disciples at the end, and only Gentiles and women are present at his death — "both outsiders in the eyes of the religious leaders, both to be the nucleus of the new community to be gathered by the risen Jesus" (Donahue 1988: 1008). This carefully crafted commentary does not venture new, "creative" views. Rather, representing the "official" stance of the corporate body of the Society of Biblical Literature, its discourse contains carefully balanced observations and judgments with a goal of representing current "accepted" scholarly opinion. Within this context, the author is free to give his own best judgments about the evidence.

A notable *action set*, namely, a group of women who coordinated their actions to achieve a particular goal, produced a one-volume commentary on the Bible in 1992 entitled *The Women's Bible Commentary*. The women editors chose Mary Ann Tolbert to enact the goals of this action set with reference to the Gospel of Mark. In contrast to the ideology guiding the Society of Biblical Literature volume, the ideology guiding the women's commentary encourages

Tolbert to entertain creative possibilities rather than simply to balance current "credible" scholarly debate. Adopting this mode, Tolbert suggests that "it is not impossible that the author [of the Gospel of Mark] was female," since the portrayal of Peter is very negative and "literacy among women had risen slightly during the period when the Gospel was written." Emphasizing that the place of final composition is unknown, she mentions Rome and Egypt as cities discussed in church tradition and moves immediately to people who lived in "large, multi-national urban areas around the Mediterranean basin" as the natural audience for the Gospel (Tolbert 1992: 264). In these areas, women of various status — of the Roman aristocracy, female slaves, prostitutes, mothers, daughters, and so on — dwelled. The Gospel of Mark depicts all the women characters positively with the exception of Herodias and her daughter (6:17–28) and possibly Jesus' mother (3:31–34). This is, Tolbert indicates, "the basis for the claims of many feminist scholars that the Christian community reflected by Mark's Gospel must have contained strong women leaders and role models" (Tolbert 1992: 263).

In the commentary on the passion narrative, Tolbert turns her attention first to the maid of the high priest who, through question-and-answer, creates the context for Peter's repeated denial of Jesus (14:66–72). Though not called a slave, this young girl has lowly status, "for no woman or girl of honorable rank would be permitted access" to the bystanders in the courtyard or would speak to Peter in public or draw public attention to herself as she does. The action and speech of this woman create a context where Jesus is speaking the truth to the high priest about his identity while Peter tells repeated lies about his. Thus, "[i]n typical Markan fashion, the anonymous, lowly, and marginal character stands for truth while the high status, powerful character rejects the truth or tells lies" (Tolbert 1992: 273). Second, Tolbert turns to the women at the cross and the tomb (15:40–16:8). These women, who have not appeared previously in the story, suddenly appear on the scene as disciples superior to the twelve who have fled, betrayed, and denied Jesus. With the presence of these three women, "the audience might have reason to hope that Jesus will finally be well served by some of his human followers" (Tolbert 1992: 273). The narrative, however, depicts all three "as conventional women of some status," identifying each woman by name. When these women hear about the resurrection, they, in the mode of the twelve disciples, flee and tell no one anything out of their fear. Thus, the women fail "to act boldly and courageously on their divine commission." Either behaving conventionally or concerning themselves with "social status, power, or customary roles," they do not become fruitful disciples. The Gospel of Mark "demands followers who are willing to act outside the constraints of society, religiously and socially." Even these women do not do this. The reader is left to fulfill this task. "At the end and indeed *by means of* the end itself, the audience of the Gospel of Mark, both women and men, are challenged to become themselves faithful disciples, carrying the message to the world, doing what some characters in the Gospel have not proved worthy to do because of their subservience to social conventions or their desires for status, wealth, fame, or power" (Tolbert 1992: 274).

Surely a fascinating aspect of this commentary is its sensitive reading of the text within the ideological guidelines of an "action set" within current scholarly circles. The reader of Tolbert's commentary is able to see significantly common insights into the inner texture and intertexture of the Gospel of Mark in the context of allegiance to significantly different goals within the commentary. A different ideology, then, has not taken the commentator away from careful, systematic reading of the text. The ideology of the action set has, however, more openly identified areas where we do not have certain knowledge, focused on aspects of the narrative that do not regularly attract attention in commentary, and entertained possibilities that would be considered too adventurous or speculative within the ideology of the larger corporately sanctioned group for which Donahue wrote.

The commentary by Ched Myers mentioned above represents yet a third alternative. The author's preface and acknowledgments indicate an ideology shared by a network of *cliques, gangs, action sets,* and *factions* in various parts of the world, all committed to "liberation reading of scripture." His commentary is "pitched half way between the deeply alienated camps of professional biblical scholarship and 'lay' Bible study" (Myers 1988: xxv). Free from a commitment to write according to the guidelines either of a corporate group or a particular action set, Myers presents a case for composition of the Gospel between June 68 and April 70 by an author who reflects the ideology of a group of early Christians who were unwilling to ally themselves with any of the groups who were fighting over the leadership of the Jerusalem temple. This group of early Christians understood Jesus as enacting nonviolent resistance. Jesus, a rurally based Messiah, engages in a direct-action campaign first throughout synagogues in Galilee, then in Jerusalem. Myers's reading of the scene with the women at the cross and the tomb is very similar to Tolbert's (or hers is similar to his, which was earlier). In addition to focusing on the women, he calls attention to various social and political issues in the story. Only in a description of Barabbas, Myers observes, does Markan discourse use "the explicit language of revolution." Markan discourse "dramatize[s] the choice" between Jesus and Barabbas by describing Barabbas as "a Sicarius terrorist" (Myers 1988: 380). When Simon the Cyrenian is "pressed into service" as he is coming in "from the fields," the discourse reminds the reader "once more of the spatial (geopolitical) tension between city/country and center/periphery" (Myers 1988: 385). Myers observes that Markan discourse distinguishes between "the 'revolutionary' Barabbas" and the "social bandits" between whom Jesus is crucified. For Myers, "Mark is making a very important ideological statement here." The discourse in Mark 13, according to Myers, "dissociate[s] Jesus from the means and ends of the rebel cause. Yet he shares their fate, as a common opponent to both Rome and the socio-economic status quo. Jesus is traded for a Sicarius, taken for a social bandit; of all the factions in Palestine, Mark situates Jesus alongside *these*" (Myers 1988: 387). Following this mode of interpretation, Myers sees the centurion at the foot of the cross as remaining in character as a Roman oppressor, rather than being a converted Christian who confesses the true nature of Jesus. For Myers, the centurion's statement that Jesus was "son of God" has the resonance of the statements of demons and political opponents previously in the discourse (3:11; 5:7; 6:3; 14:71). "In other words, the title does not represent a 'confession' at all, but more often the hostile response of those struggling to gain power over Jesus by 'naming' him.... Rome has triumphed over the Nazarene, he has been 'named' by the executioner who pronounces him 'dead' (15:44f.)" (Myers 1988: 394). It is not that the centurion is squarely in the context of taunting, ironic speech, like the chief priests and scribes who sneer at Jesus with the title "Messiah, King of Israel" (15:32). Rather, the centurion, along with demons, the high priest, and Pilate, "'know who Jesus is,' and are out to destroy him, whereas those who follow him are often unsure who he is, but struggle to trust him nevertheless" (Myers 1988: 394). Because, as observed above, the women fail to tell the message about Jesus after his death, "the only reliable postexecution 'witness' to Jesus will be a "young man," who tells the women that Jesus is alive and that the discipleship adventure will continue" (Myers 1988: 394).

The ideological goals of Myers's commentary, then, create a freedom to read Markan discourse through the eyes of one who himself has stood with three others "one cold morning at the Pentagon, Thanksgiving 1976" (Myers 1988: xxxii). Again, many of the inner textual and intertextual features he observes in the text are the same as those commented upon by Donahue and Tolbert. But the ideological texture of his discourse has significantly more social and political body than theirs. Tolbert's commentary explores the presence of women's bodies in the discourse more than Donahue's commentary. But still her commentary is characterized by social and political restraint. Myers's commentary, in contrast, adopts an ideological mode that observes every social and political issue he can find in the discourse and explores the possible meanings of those issues in the context of Markan discourse from the beginning of the story to its end.

C. Modes of Intellectual Discourse

In 1975, John Gager raised the issue of ideology in the interpretation of early Christian texts. Asserting that conflict reaches its most intense level when it involves competing ideologies or competing views of the same ideology, he presented three critical moments in the history of early Christianity:

a. conflict with Judaism over the claim to represent the true Israel;

b. conflict with paganism over the claim to possess true wisdom;

c. conflict among Christian groups over the claim to embody the authen-
    tic faith of Jesus and the apostles. (Gager 1975: 82)

In addition, he proposed that the intensity of the struggles was a function
of two separate factors:

a. the degree to which individuals considered themselves to be members
    of a group, so that any threat to the group became a threat to every
    individual;

b. the role of intellectuals who transformed personal motivations into
    eternal truths. (Gager 1975: 82)

Gager uses the term "ideology" alternatively with the phrase "symbolic
universe" (Gager 1975: 83). For an institution, an ideology integrates "different provinces of meaning" and encompasses "the institutional order in a
symbolic totality"; for an individual, it "puts everything in its right place"
(Gager 1975: 82; using Berger and Luckmann 1967: 95, 98).

•

An interpreter's adoption of a mode of theological, historical, sociological,
anthropological, psychological, or literary discourse for commentary is a significant matter, since a mode of intellectual discourse is a particular mode of
social production. Each intellectual mode of interaction and exchange has a
relation to an ideological field in the modern/postmodern world in which we
live (Eagleton 1991).

1. Historical-Critical Discourse

First, let us look at an example of narrative analysis that is ideologically
aligned with historical-critical interpretation. Here the discourse adopts the
mode of accurate historiography that yields theological insight into God's
activity in the world. It is fair to say that this kind of discourse currently
dominates most commentaries on New Testament texts:

> When the false witnesses accuse him [Jesus] of threatening to destroy
> the temple and promising to build another, their witness is patently
> false. Jesus never said that he would destroy the temple. But by the
> cursing of the fig tree and his final discourse, he does announce its de-
> struction. On a level that Jesus' persecutors cannot understand, there
> is truth in the temple charge. By his death, Jesus makes the old temple
> and its cultic worship obsolete. In its place, he establishes a new com-
> munity of believers: Jews and Gentiles, a temple not made by human
> hands. (Matera 1986: 72)

Matera says his account does not try to present a historical study: "that is, it does not try to reconstruct the historical events which actually occurred" (Matera 1986: 5). The goal "is to study each passion narrative in terms of the particular evangelist's theology" (Matera 1986: 6). Since Matera's discourse is sound and sober "narrative" theology, however, the ideological texture of the commentary evokes a certainty that the reader is getting a basically accurate insight into the history of first-century Christianity. Only if the theology were radical or excessive would the history be unreliable. Or to put it another way, the discourse evokes a conviction that there is really no better insight into this history than these texts that were chosen by reputable early Christians to represent the story of who they are. As indicated above, this mode of discourse represents dominant culture rhetoric in the field of biblical studies today. But there are also modes of discourse with significantly different ideological alliances.

2. Social-Scientific Criticism

Another mode of discourse that has developed during the last quarter of a century emerges from social-scientific criticism. Here is some of the discourse produced by Bruce Malina and Richard Rohrbaugh on Mark 15 in this mode:

> In all of the Gospels [Jesus' opponents destroy his standing in the eyes of the people] through what anthropologists call "status degradation rituals," by which is meant a process of publicly recasting, relabeling, humiliating, and thus recategorizing a person as a social deviant. . . . The attempts of many to treat [Mark 15:1–20] as a "legal" trial notwithstanding (frequently citing the regulations of the Mishnah for the conduct of criminal cases even though there is little attempt here to "prove" criminality), Mark and the other evangelists portray these events as a public ritual of humiliation aimed at destroying the status that until now had given Jesus credibility in the eyes of the public. (Malina and Rohrbaugh 1992: 272–73)

This discourse aligns itself with anthropologists and focuses on "pivotal values" like honor and shame and common perceptions like patron-client and kinship relationships, limited good, hospitality, and purity in the Mediterranean world (Malina 1993; Elliott 1993; Neyrey 1991). The discourse invests itself most directly with social and cultural anthropologists, with a special commitment to overcoming ethnocentrism and anachronism. The leadership of this group of interpreters grew out of the Catholic Biblical Association, and they have established this mode of commentary in the Society of Biblical Literature with both national and international practitioners. The ideological texture of this discourse locates a person among social scientists rather than literary critics or theologians.

3. History-of-Religions Discourse

The work of Mircea Eliade during the twentieth century has created history-of-religions discourse that stands in contrast both to theological-historical and social-scientific discourse. This discourse, like social-scientific criticism, uses historical-anthropological resources, but it uses them to compare religious rituals, myths, festivals, and practices in groups anywhere in the world. Jonathan Z. Smith is a historian of religions who has worked closely both with New Testament scholars and with the texts of early Christianity. Let us look briefly at the ideological texture of some of his commentary:

> A "gospel" is a narrative of a son of god who appears among men as a riddle inviting misunderstanding. I would want to claim the title "gospel" for the *Vitae* attributed to Mark and John as well as for those by Philostratus [about Apollonius of Tyana] and Iamblichus [about Pythagoras]....I am not describing a shift from myth (i.e. "aretalogy") to *kerygma* or a process of existential demythologization. I would want to insist, as an historian of religions, that what I have attempted to describe is thoroughly consistent with a proper understanding of myth....
> I would propose that there is no such category as "pristine" myth but only application and that this application derives from the character of myth as a self-conscious category mistake....My understanding of the nature of application has been much influenced by recent anthropological studies of divination....Myth as narrative...is an analogue to the limited number of objects manipulated by the diviner. Myth as application represents the complex interaction between diviner, client and "situation." There is delight and there is play in both the "fit" and the incongruity of the "fit," between an element in the myth and this or that segment of the world that one has encountered. (Smith 1978: 204–6)

Viewed from Smith's perspective, Matera's theological-historical commentary makes an intellectual mistake that no commentator should make as he or she interprets the Gospel of Mark — namely, it does not recognize that Markan discourse is myth as narrative. The social-scientific commentary of Malina and Rohrbaugh, on the other hand, basically bypasses the nature of Mark as religious text to explicate it as a social and cultural text. The inner nature of the discourse, for Smith, is to intertwine a belief in God who has the final say over humans with the life of a person who engaged in radical enough activity to get himself killed in Jerusalem — a major ritual, political, and economic center of Jewish life during the first century. The challenge Smith envisions is to figure out the manner in which the "two stories" (myth and "life of") play with each other to create the incongruous story the text itself calls "gospel." For Smith, the issue is not the relation between story and discourse, as literary critics often suggest. For a historian of religion, a primary issue is the application of myth to the "life of" a particular person (a *vita*).

4. New Historical Discourse

Burton Mack enacts this history-of-religions approach to New Testament texts in a mode of discourse perhaps most accurately described as postmodern "new historical" commentary (see Veeser 1989; Thomas 1991). Mack uses the insights both of historians of religion like Jonathan Z. Smith and of postmodern critics like Jacques Derrida and Michel Foucault to generate a new historiography of first-century Christianity. For him, the Markan account of the death of Jesus is a "moment" in the creation of early Christian historiography. Early Christians create their "history" by interrelating myth and "lives of" Jesus in highly complex and multivalent ways.

> Jesus' death [in Mark] is the sign of the end of the temple's time. The rending of the temple curtain anticipates the destruction of the temple in 70 C.E. There is no other sense to be made of the concentration of suggestions than that the reader associate the two events. Apocalyptic mentality would have understood the destruction of the temple as an act of God's judgment in any case. Mark stacked up the reasons for seeing it related to the crucifixion of Jesus. The reason he could not make the point explicit in a direct statement is because to have named a single cause either of the crucifixion or of the temple's destruction would have ruined the multimotivational interpretation of the events he had in mind and the reciprocal dynamics of conflict he needed in order to carry out his fiction. (Mack 1988: 297)

Mack's discourse participates ideologically in intellectual circles that produce history-of-religions commentary informed by critical anthropology. These ideological commitments have a significantly different social and cultural location than the commitments of people who produce either theological or social-scientific commentary. The goal of understanding the nature of Christianity as a religion among all other religions is significantly different from a goal of understanding Christianity as the one religion that, with its own discourse, appropriately informs a person's view of the world. Also, it differs from a use of the social sciences to analyze a text as a social and cultural text rather than a religious text. Smith and Mack quite consciously select discourse that is different both from Christian discourse informed primarily by theological terminology and from social-science discourse that is not addressed to religious phenomena as a way to shed light on the nature of Christian discourse. Smith and Mack use both social-science discourse that focuses on religious phenomena and literary discourse that focuses on religious texts to analyze the Gospel of Mark. Only a certain group of interpreters invest their discourse in this kind of commentary.

5. Postmodern Deconstructive Discourse

There is yet another postmodern form of discourse on the current scene. Stephen Moore vigorously enacts postmodern discourse in the mode of postmodern literary critics who perform "deconstruction" rather than the discipline of history of religions. Here is a sample:

> Tolbert is surely right [that the women in Mark 15:40–41 depict a group similar to but much better than the Twelve]. But is excellence rewarded in the Marcan workplace? Mark is hardly a manifesto for equal-opportunity employment. Jesus' final message addressed to the eleven, collected by the mysterious young (mail)man and carried to the tomb or office where everything *should* be sorted (out), threatens to become yet another card adrift in a bag, yet another victim of a strike or a sorting accident. And thanks to whom? Mark's female postal workers? Mark has used his author-ity over these women to place them in a compromising position. His(s)tory recounts that they resigned without notice just when they were most needed. (Moore 1992: 45)

Instead of creating a context in which the Gospel of Mark functions as religious text alongside other religious texts in antiquity, Moore creates a context in modern culture where people send and receive postcards. The ideological texture of Moore's discourse is allied with intellectuals in universities throughout the world who produce poststructuralist, deconstructive literary commentary as a social product. Rather than investing their time with religious phenomena in antiquity, they devote their energies to phenomena that appear in modern and postmodern media. Here the issue is the Gospel of Mark as a written text in the context of other media in the world in which we live today. What kind of medium of communication and action is the Gospel of Mark? Selecting this mode of discourse for commentary on the Gospel of Mark gives an interpreter access to very different social and economic circles of production than the theological mode Matera enacts, the social-scientific mode Malina and Rohrbaugh enact, or the history-of-religions mode Smith enacts. Since Mack also aligns his commentary with postmodern discourse, his commentary finds an open door to some of the same social and economic circles of production of discourse as Moore's.

D. Spheres of Ideology

Ideology, as mentioned above, concerns people's relationship to other people. But ideology does not just concern people; it concerns the discourse of people. The term "ideology" "represents the points where power impacts upon certain utterances and inscribes itself tacitly within them" (Eagleton 1991: 223). Thus, a discussion of ideology must move to texts, which contain human language — "signs" on a printed page into which are inscribed both "discursive" and "non-discursive" practices (Eagleton 1991: 219). Texts contain accounts of nondiscursive practices, like "dislodging a pebble from one's left ear" (Eagleton 1991: 219). But they also contain accounts of discursive practices, like a galley slave being required to row "non-stop for fifteen hours at a stretch and sending up a feeble chant of praise to the Emperor on the hour" (Eagleton 1991: 206). Thus, there are ways to analyze the ideological texture of a text. Three of these ways are: analyzing the social and cultural location of the implied author of the text; analyzing the ideology of power in the discourse of the text; and analyzing the ideology in the mode of intellectual discourse both in the text and in the interpretation of the text.

I. Ideology in the Social and Cultural Location of the Implied Author

A way to begin to build insight into the ideological texture of a text is to analyze the spectrum of social and cultural data the implied author of the text builds into the language of the text. These data exhibit the social and cultural location of the implied author (Robbins 1991a: 305–32). A taxonomy of nine items, developed by T. H. Carney (1975), provides an excellent framework for this analysis (cf. Neyrey 1993: 32–41, 128–41).

a. Previous events. Mark 15 is based in part on the following data regarding previous events: at some time in the past Jerusalem had become a center of power with official roles designated for chief priests, elders, and scribes; by some process a council had been either appointed or elected to make official decisions concerning issues that included people's actions; officials in Rome had decided to appoint a prefect to reside in Jerusalem and oversee the people's activity to assure peace and order in the city, and they had appointed Pilate in that office; at some time in the past, an entire battalion of the Roman army had been sent to Jerusalem to reside there and be at the disposal of Pilate to keep order (15:16); and just previous to the events in this chapter, a group of Jewish men had caused a disturbance that included murder and had been charged with insurrection and put in prison (15:7).

In contrast to these official, public events, a group of women had followed Jesus when he was in Galilee, ministering to him. Recently, they had accompanied Jesus when he came up to Jerusalem prior to the beginning of Passover. Also, some time in the past someone had hewn a tomb out of a rock in which someone could be buried (15:46).

b. Natural environment and resources. The Roman soldiers have a purple cloak in their possession, and thorns are nearby for making a crown (15:17). Also, they have access to a reed (15:19) and wood to build a cross (15:21). In addition, they have wine and myrrh (15:23). Bystanders have access to a sponge, reed, and vinegar (15:36). Joseph of Arimathea is able to procure linen cloth in which to wrap Jesus' body. Spices for anointing a corpse are available in the city for purchase with money (16:1).

c. Population structure. The discourse in this chapter has in view a population of the city that includes chief priests, elders, scribes, a Roman prefect, centurions, soldiers, a Cyrenian who works in the country, and women. The remaining population is an undifferentiated mass of people. The discourse does not mention children, and it does not differentiate among day workers, artisans, and so on. Thus, the discourse envisions a large number of people with vested authority and a mass of undifferentiated people.

d. *Technology.* People have the technology to build a palace (15:16), to make a purple cloak (15:20), to make a cross (15:21), to make wine (15:23) and vinegar (15:36), to make a large curtain for the temple (15:38), to make linen cloth (15:46), to hew a tomb out of a rock (15:46), and to make money (15:46; 16:1).

e. *Socialization and personality.* Jewish temple leaders, crowds of people, and members of the council have access to the Roman prefect Pilate (15:1, 8, 43). Pilate is able to converse with a Galilean Jew, with crowds in Jerusalem, with a member of the Jerusalem council, and, of course, with a centurion (15:2, 8–14, 43–45).

f. *Culture:* The discourse has significant Jewish culture and Roman culture in view, and it mentions the presence of rural culture (15:21).

g. *Foreign affairs.* There is general awareness that the Roman government is focused enough on Jerusalem that it orders a prefect and a battalion of soldiers to be present in the city.

h. *Belief systems and ideologies.* The discourse has a concept of King of the Jews (15:2, 9, 12, 18, 26), Messiah, King of Israel (15:32), God (15:34), Elijah (15:35), and son of God (15:39). Also, there is a cultural tradition of a Passover festival (15:6), of paying homage to a king (15:19), of crucifying bandits and revolutionaries (15:26–27), of the sabbath (15:42), of anointing a corpse with spices (16:1), of wrapping a corpse in linen cloth and burying it in a hewn-out rock (15:46), and of resurrection (16:6).

i. *Political-military-legal system.* There is a dominant presence of a political-military-legal system in this discourse.

•

All of this means that the implied author of this discourse envisions Jerusalem as an urban center dominated by both temple hierarchy and Roman officials and military personnel. Ched Myers has argued that the implied author presents an assault on the city and its leaders from the margins of the wilderness and countryside. The overall movement of the narrative begins with revelation in the wilderness and presents cycles of campaigns on the geopolitical spaces of cities.

In the context of the Jewish-Roman Wars of 66–70, the Gospel of Mark exhibits the tensions of followers of Jesus as a Jewish movement caught in the middle of intensive infighting over the Jerusalem temple and its leadership. As Jewish discourse, the Gospel of Mark represents a Messianite group that refuses to join any of the groups that engage in military action against another to "reinstate" traditional leadership or establish a new base for leadership.

2. Ideology of Power in the Discourse of the Text

Foucault's guidelines for analyzing power relations in a text (Castelli 1991: 50, 122) appeared as an afterword in a major study of Foucault's work (Dreyfus and Rabinow 1983: 208–26). Elizabeth Castelli's summary yields the following principles:

a. Define the *system of differentiations* that allows dominant people to act upon the actions of people in a subordinate position.

b. Articulate the *types of objectives* held by those who act upon the actions of others.

c. Identify the *means* for bringing these relationships into being.

d. Identify the *forms of institutionalization of power.*

e. Analyze the *degree of rationalization* of power relations.

A dominant mode of discourse in Mark 15 differentiates between people who give orders and people who carry out those orders. Pilate orders soldiers to crucify Jesus, and they do. Soldiers order Simon the Cyrenian to carry Jesus' cross, and he does. The young man in the tomb orders the women to go and tell Peter and the disciples about the empty tomb and the resurrection of Jesus. Perhaps another mode is properly called "request," but the social dynamics of a request are dependent on the person who issues it. The temple hierarchy requests that Pilate do something with Jesus; the crowd requests that Pilate crucify Jesus and release Barabbas. Pilate requests that Jesus tell him if he is King of the Jews, and he requests information from the centurion who remained at the cross where Jesus was crucified. Joseph requests the corpse of Jesus so he can bury it.

The objective of chief priests, scribes, elders, Pilate, centurions, and soldiers in Mark 15 is to gain or maintain power over other people in that setting. The objective of the women is to maintain an "honorable" relation to a person whom they have followed and served for a significant period of time. The objective of Joseph of Arimathea is either to honor Jesus of Nazareth or not to dishonor the sabbath by allowing a man to hang on a cross during it.

The dominant means for bringing these relationships into being are actions, giving orders, and making requests. Chief priests, scribes, and elders give orders for Jesus to be arrested. After the action of holding a trial, they take Jesus to Pilate. After Pilate interacts with a crowd of people who come to him to release a prisoner for the festival, he whips Jesus and gives orders for him to be crucified. After the soldiers mock Jesus through actions and speech, they crucify him. Joseph of Arimathea goes to Pilate and requests the corpse of Jesus, and Pilate, after he sends for the centurion and receives verification that Jesus is dead, gives permission to Joseph to bury Jesus' corpse. Joseph takes Jesus' body down from the cross, wraps it in linen cloth, and buries it in a tomb. Women buy spices and come to the tomb after the sabbath to anoint the corpse. The young man in the tomb announces the resurrection of Jesus and gives the women orders to go and tell Peter and the disciples what they have seen and heard.

The forms of institutionalization and power are the temple, the Jewish court, the Roman military establishment, and the office of prefect in Jerusalem. Markan discourse, then, presents two dominant institutional forms in Jerusalem.

The rationalization of the activity in Mark 15 is highly complex and conflicted. The temple hierarchy responds with rage to Jesus' answer to the high priest's question if he is the Messiah, the Son of the Blessed (14:61–65). The narrator asserts that Pilate perceived the chief priests had handed Jesus over out of envy (15:10), and the chief priests and scribes may be acting out this motive in their taunt that he saved others but cannot save himself (15:31). The inscription of the charge against Jesus read, "The King of the Jews" (15:26). Jesus provides the rationale for his death in scripture (9:12; 14:21) and "God's will" (8:31; 14:36). Just before he dies, Jesus cries out that God has forsaken him. Was it necessary for God to forsake Jesus at the moment of death so that God could cause Jesus to rise up from death?

The ideology of power in Mark 15, then, is highly complex. There can be no wonder that commentators with widely different ideological alignments can have a feeding frenzy at its table. In the words of Jonathan Z. Smith:

> Whether revealed in a characteristic form of spells: "You are this, you are not this, you are that" "It is I, it is not I, it is so and so who says this" or in the equally characteristic use in the biographical tradition of riddle, aporia, joke and parable, these figures depend upon a multivalent expression which is interpreted by admirers and detractors as having univocal meaning and thus invites, again by admirers and detractors alike, misunderstanding. The function of the narrative is to play between various levels of understanding and misunderstanding, inviting the reader to assume that both he and the author truly do understand and then cutting the ground out from under this confidence. The figure for whom the designation son of god is claimed characteristically plays with our seriousness and is most serious when he appears to be playing. This is a sign of his freedom and transcendence, the *sine qua non* of a religious figure of Late Antiquity worthy of belief. (Smith 1978: 194)

What mode of intellectual discourse will you choose for your production of commentary on biblical texts? The mode you choose will give a particular ideological texture to your discourse. This ideological texture will align you with certain intellectual circles and estrange you from others. Most of all, the tension between the mode you choose (or the mode that chooses you) and the life you live will make life exciting and interesting, or this tension will turn biblical interpretation into a form of work from which you feel progressively more alienated as you increase in years. My wish for you is that the ideological texture of your discourse be so comfortable to you that you cannot perceive yourself communicating in any other way than you do to your colleagues and friends throughout the world. If biblical interpretation is serious, it is fun. If it is not fun, it is nothing at all worthy of doing in the sight of God.

STUDY GUIDE:
Ideological Texture — The Ethiopian Eunuch

This study guide concerns the ideological texture of interpretations of Acts 8:26–40, which tells about an Ethiopian eunuch who, after traveling to Jerusalem to worship, meets and talks with Philip during his return home to Ethiopia. Clarice J. Martin, who was the only African-American woman in the United States with a Ph.D. in New Testament studies during the 1980s, published an interpretation of this story in 1989 that showed how traditional scholarship regularly bypasses the issue of the Ethiopian identity of this early convert to Christianity.

The procedure of this study guide is to work directly with the text in Acts itself and to supply information Martin discusses in her essay.

•

1. Read Acts 8:26–40 through from beginning to end. Describe the actions of Philip in the story. Why is Philip on this particular road? Why does Philip go over to the chariot of the Ethiopian and talk to him? What happens to Philip after his time with the Ethiopian? What do these aspects of the story tell you about the nature of this story?

2. Reread Acts 8:27. Describe all the features the narration describes about the Ethiopian. Martin indicates that a number of interpreters call the traveler a "chamberlain" and that the most appropriate definition for its application to the man in this story is "a steward of a king or queen" (Martin 1989: 105).

3. Martin suggests that one of the most fully explored aspects of the text is its "theological" dimensions. The first of these dimensions concerns the Lukan emphasis on the role of the Holy Spirit in preaching and evangelism (Luke 4:18; 24:44; Acts 1:8; 4:8–10; 7:55; 10:11–12; 13:4–10; 16:6–7). Identify the three verses in the story about the Ethiopian that exhibit this emphasis and explain their relation to the passages in Luke and Acts.

The second topic is the "witness" of early Christians to the significance of the events of Jesus' life, death, and resurrection. Identify the verses in the Ethiopian story that are related to witness in Luke 1:1–4; 24:48; Acts

1:21–22; 4:33; 10:39–41; 22:14–15 and explain their significance in the overarching story.

The third topic is the "joy" of the Ethiopian in relation to his conversion experience. Identify the verse of special importance in the story that relates to Luke 1:44; 2:10; 15:4–7; 19:6, 37; 24:41; Acts 2:47; 8:8; 11:18; 16:33.

The fourth topic is "prophecy-fulfillment" or "proof from prophecy." Describe the relation of the story to prophecy-fulfillment as it applies to Isa 53:7–12.

4. Martin observes that these rich studies of the theological texture of the story either ignore or deny the importance of the man's identity as an Ethiopian. F. D. Gealy, for example, admits that the man is an "Ethiopian" and an "outlander," but he argues that Luke avoids any attention to this identity and concludes that "his ethnic origin is strictly underdetermined" (Martin 1989: 110, quoting Gealy 1962: 177–78). Nils Dahl directly cautions the reader against concluding that the Ethiopian is black:

> What made his conversion to be remembered and told as a legend was neither his African provenance nor his black skin. (It is quite possible that he was black, but that is never said . . .). In the Lucan composition this story has been placed between the evangelization among the Samaritans and the vocation of Paul, preparing for the mission to the Gentiles. Thus we get a picture of a progressive widening of the circle reached by the gospel; but the question of nationality has no special importance. (Martin 1989: 110, quoting Dahl 1974: 62–73)

Do you think these are sufficient interpretations of the narrational identity of the man as an Ethiopian in Acts 8:27?

5. Martin counters these interpretations through a number of steps. First, she works intertextually with prophecy and fulfillment between the Old Testament and this story. Read Isa 56:3–7 and interpret its relation to the journey of the Ethiopian to Jerusalem in Acts 8:27. Martin explains that the fulfillment of Isa 56:3–7 abolishes the forbidding of the entrance of eunuchs into the assembly of God in Deut 23:1. Read Ps 68:31 and explain how an understanding of this verse as prophecy would add yet another specific dimension of fulfillment to the story.

6. Second, Martin works with social and cultural intertexture. A text of Homer describes Odysseus's Ethiopian herald as follows: "He was round shouldered, dark of skin, and curly-haired, and his name was Eurybates" (*Odyssey* 19.244–48). Seneca, a Roman writer (4 B.C.E.–65 C.E.), describes Ethiopians in this manner: "First of all, the burnt color of the people indicates that Ethiopia is very hot" (Seneca *Naturales Questiones* 4A. 218). In a context of additional information from artistic descriptions and other data from antiquity, Martin quotes the conclusion of a modern scholar:

> Blackness and the Ethiopian were . . . in many respects synonymous. . . . The Ethiopian's blackness became proverbial, and gave rise to the

expression..."to wash an Ethiopian white...." Ethiopians were the yardstick by which antiquity measured colored peoples. The skin of the Ethiopian was black, in fact, blacker, it was noted, than that of any other people. Indians were dark or black — the Indians whom Alexander visited were said to be blacker than the rest of mankind with the exception of Ethiopians. (Martin 1989: 111, quoting Snowden 1979: 5, 23)

Do you think Martin is right to question traditional interpretations that suggest that the term "Ethiopian" had no special national meaning in Acts?

7. Third, Martin works with maps of "the New Testament world." She was able to find only one Bible atlas that includes Meroë, the capital of Ethiopia (or Nubia), in a map of the New Testament world. Do you find it on any map either for the Old or New Testament in your Bible or in a textbook available to you? Martin calls the absence of this location on biblical maps a "politics of omission" in biblical scholarship. Do you think this criticism is justified? The ancient writer Strabo (ca. 64 B.C.E.–19 C.E.) identifies Ethiopia as the southernmost region of the world (Martin 1989: 119). Do you think it is appropriate, then, to interpret the last clause in Acts 1:8 as being fulfilled in the Ethiopian's journey down to his homeland rather than in Paul's journey to Rome in Acts 27–28?

8. Toward the end of her essay, Martin states that in order for the interpretation of biblical traditions to be "interpretation for liberation" of people it must be as balanced and open as possible to all nationalities, races, and marginalized people who come into view in biblical texts. Would you agree with this statement or disagree with it?

9. Martin does not include any detailed analysis of the Ethiopian as a eunuch. Can you see any reason why this aspect of the Ethiopian's identity would not be of special interest to Martin? Can you imagine any reason why Martin may not want to discuss in detail this aspect of his identity? Do you think that all of us may, either wittingly or unwittingly, omit or overlook certain aspects of New Testament texts in our interpretations of them? Explain the reasons for such omissions in a balanced way that is fair to her as well as your own and other people's interpretations.

STUDY GUIDE:
Ideological Texture — Women Keep Silent

This study guide explores the ideological dimension of selected texts in 1 Corinthians. When exploring ideology, one can focus on the ideology present in the text itself or on how the ideology of the interpreter(s) is borne out. In this study guide we will be dealing with the ideology of the text.

The rise of ideological criticism has paralleled the greater prominence of women and/or minority voices in scholarship. Looking "underneath" the text for the interests that are supported by certain modes of discourse has allowed readers of the Bible to see New Testament texts in a new light. For instance, the New Testament was written in a patriarchal society, and the language about women in the New Testament reflects its patriarchal roots. Feminist criticism, which often takes the form of ideological criticism, has been especially helpful in highlighting the muted portraits and voices of women in both the Old and New Testaments.

When a person reads for the ideological aspects of a text, he or she seeks to find both the interests of the author and how those interests are argued. As Terry Eagleton says, "the concept of ideology aims to disclose something of the relation between an utterance and its material conditions of possibility, when those conditions of possibility are viewed in the light of certain power-struggles central to the reproduction . . . of a whole form of social life" (Eagleton 1991: 223). Ideological criticism thus is closely tied to investigation of the social location of the author and how that author is situated vis-à-vis the audience and the culture.

Paul's statements about women in 1 Corinthians provide an excellent case for ideological criticism for at least two reasons. First, they deal with a certain power dynamic both in Paul's culture and in the history of the church — the relationship between men and women. Throughout the letter Paul forcefully sets forth his point of view, and by taking a stance on the place of women in the church, he enters into the cultural conversation about gender. Second, in 1 Corinthians we find Paul asserting certain tenets about the role of women that may not cohere with other texts in Paul and thus may more blatantly display his underlying ideology than other passages.

•

1. Read 1 Cor 14:26–40. What is the main point of Paul's argument with respect to worship? What do you think seems to be the problem with the Corinthians' actions when they are assembled together? (It will be helpful here to compare 14:3 and 14:6–9.) What does Paul's view of worship imply about his view of the church?

2. Now look again at 14:33–36. How do these verses function within the larger context of Paul's argument? Why does Paul suddenly introduce women into his discussion? Some scholars have thought that these verses were a later addition to this letter that reflect the viewpoint expressed in 1 Tim 2:11–15. What would be the reasons for assuming that these verses are an insertion? How might you argue that they fit with this passage?

Most scholars think that 1 Timothy was written at a time period when church order was more advanced. Compare the role of women in 1 Corinthians to that in 1 Timothy. How has the prominence of women increased or decreased? Can you find in the text reasons for this change?

3. In an earlier passage, Paul has talked about the role of women with

respect to how they dress in the worship assembly. Read 1 Cor 11:2–16. Try to paraphrase or outline this difficult explanation of why women should keep their heads covered. What is the theological or christological basis for women covering their heads while men leave theirs uncovered? Does this rationale seem to be a unified, logical support for Paul's position? If not, where does it break down?

4. The prophetesses in the Greco-Roman world usually gave their oracles in an ecstatic manner with their hair flowing freely as they spoke. Furthermore, women with unbraided, loose hair might be associated with prostitution. How do these facets of Paul's social world help explain his comments in 11:2–16? What is his ultimate conclusion about how women should act in worship, and what are his reasons for this conclusion?

5. Finally, these two passages need to be read alongside other of Paul's comments both in 1 Corinthians and in other passages. Compare Gal 3:28–29; 1 Cor 1:11; 7:13; Rom 13:1–3; 16:1–2. Can you make any generalizations about Paul's attitude toward the role of women in the church and in society? How do 1 Cor 11:2–16 and 14:33–36 support or hinder an attempt to make a blanket statement about Paul's view of women? In particular, what power dynamics are at work in these passages, and what sort of interests is Paul promoting here?

Chapter 5

Sacred Texture

SEEKING THE DIVINE IN A TEXT

People who read the New Testament regularly are interested in finding insights into the nature of the relation between human life and the divine. In other words, these readers are interested in locating the ways the text speaks about God or gods, or talks about realms of religious life. The study of the sacred texture of a text has a long history. Throughout the centuries, interpreters have developed both systematic and creative ways to explore texts regarding their holy, divine nature. The following categories represent an attempt to guide the reader in a programmatic search for sacred aspects of a text, whether or not the text is scriptural. There are no references to commentaries or articles in this chapter, since the reader will be able to find basic information about the sacred texture of any biblical text in scholarly publications in any good college or seminary library.

A. Deity

God, or divine being, may exist either in the background or in a direct position of action and speech in a text. This is the realm of theology par excellence — the nature of God and God's action and revelation. Sometimes there is simply reference to God or a god in a text. Sometimes God speaks and acts like another character in the story. Describing the nature of God can be a first step toward analyzing and interpreting the sacred texture of a text.

Mark 15:1–16:8 contains a double reference to God when Jesus, dying on the cross, cries out, "My God, my God, why have you forsaken me?" It is noticeable that there is no vocal response by God, as there often is in the Hebrew Bible. After Jesus' baptism, a voice from heaven (God's voice) says, "You are my beloved son; with you I am well pleased" (Mark 1:11). At Jesus' transfiguration, a voice comes out of the cloud that overshadows Jesus, saying, "This is my beloved son; listen to him" (9:7). Thus, God does speak twice in the Gospel of Mark. Why does God not speak to Jesus while he is dying on the cross? Does this mean that God does not hear or respond to Jesus' cry?

God also does not speak when Jesus prays to God in Gethsemane saying, "Abba, father, all things are possible to you; remove this cup from me; yet not what I will, but what you will" (14:36). Jesus' speech in this setting asserts that God is Jesus' father. It also asserts that there is nothing this father cannot do. Everything is possible for him. In what sense is God father in the Markan narrative? There is significant imaging of God as father in the other Gospels in the New Testament, but there is very little explanation in Mark of what this might mean. Is it really the case that God the father can do all things? What the reader does see is an implication that the answer of God to Jesus is, "No, I will not remove this cup from you." The nature of God the father, then, is to allow Jesus to suffer and die. God does not remove this ordeal from Jesus. Would it be possible that God the father could remove this ordeal from his son but that he wills not to remove it?

What is the nature of God, then, as the Gospel of Mark reveals God? One of the characteristics is that God regularly does not work explicitly and openly in Mark, as God works at times in the Old Testament. God is present behind the scenes, responding favorably to Jesus at his baptism and transfiguration but otherwise not entering the story in an explicit, open manner. God also works in paradoxical ways. This means that God does things that appear to humans to be contradictory to one another. We will want to find some of the ways, then, that God is at work implicitly, perhaps secretly, and paradoxically in the Gospel of Mark.

B. Holy Person

Regularly a sacred text features one or more people who have a special relation to God or to divine powers. In New Testament texts, the holy person par excellence is Jesus the Christ. Thus, this special area of discussion in New Testament texts regularly is called christology — ways of talking about Jesus as Christ, the Messiah. The term "Christ" means a person specially chosen and appointed by God to bring humans into a saving relation to God, or perhaps to enact the punishment of people who are evil. But there are other holy persons in New Testament texts as well. Priests, Pharisees, Sadducees, and scribes have a status that associates them with holy things or holy ways. Mark presents them as inferior to Jesus. Frequently there are holy persons of higher and lower status in a text. The interaction of these people with one another creates an environment in which subtle distinctions can be made between truly authentic religious thought and behavior and beliefs and practices that are inferior.

In Mark 15:1–16:8, priests and scribes in charge of activities in the Jerusalem temple hand Jesus over to Pilate (15:1), and later they mock Jesus by taunting him to come down from the cross and save himself (15:31–32). Chief priests without the assistance of scribes convince the crowd to insist that Pilate release Barabbas and crucify Jesus (15:11–15). According to Mark, the chief priests act this way because they envy Jesus (15:10). There is, then, conflict between different kinds of people associated with holy things in the Gospel of Mark. The exceptional holy status of Jesus is emphasized through a negative characterization of officials in charge of the Jerusalem temple. The negative identity of officials in charge of holy things creates a context that heightens the image of Jesus as specially chosen to perform extraordinary acts associated with holiness and the ways of God.

Jesus, then, is a person specially chosen by God in the Gospel of Mark. The speech of the heavenly voice at Jesus' baptism and transfiguration makes this clear when it refers to Jesus as "my beloved son" (1:11; 9:7). Thus, the counterpart of God as "Abba, father" (14:36), noted above, is that Jesus is God's son. But what does it mean to be God's son? We saw above that God would not remove "the cup" of suffering and death from his son when he requested it. Why would this be? What is the nature of God's son that God will not remove suffering, rejection, and death from him?

The narrative speaks only implicitly or obliquely about the reasons why God allows his son to suffer and die. Mark 15:1–16:8, however, contains a dramatic moment that focuses on this aspect of being son of God. When the centurion standing at the foot of the cross sees Jesus die, he says, "Truly this man was son of God" (15:39). There is disagreement in interpretation concerning exactly what the centurion responded to and what his response means. The narrator says the centurion responded this way when he saw Jesus breathe his last "in this way" (15:39). What does "in this way" mean? Does it mean dying in a context of incredible suffering, rejection, and mockery? Does it mean dying in a context of alienation from God? Does it mean dying without saying anything until the moment of death? Does it mean dying in a context where the sky becomes dark and the curtain of the temple is split in two from top to bottom? Even if we cannot answer these questions with certainty, the questions themselves imply some of the meanings and meaning-effects of the centurion's assertion that Jesus was truly son of God.

After Jesus' death and burial, a young man in a white robe sitting in the tomb says that Jesus has risen and gone before the disciples to Galilee, where they will see him (16:6–7). Jesus, then, does not remain in death. The implication is that although God allowed his beloved son to die, he did not allow death to be his final state. Divine powers at work through Jesus when he was alive appear to restore life to his body after he dies. This is perhaps the ultimate acclamation in the Markan account of the status of Jesus' holiness. His life on earth was of such a special quality that death was not the final result of his life. The natural question to ask is why this specially chosen person was not spared suffering, rejection, and death. Why was he not simply given special life without dying? This question leads to other aspects of the sacred texture of the Gospel of Mark.

C. Spirit Being

Sacred texts often feature special divine or evil beings who have the nature of a spirit rather than a fully human being. The Gospel of Mark refers to angels, holy spirit, demons or unclean spirits, and the devil. The presence of these beings features competition between forces of good and evil. The sacred texture of a text often emerges in the context of conflict between good and evil spiritual forces. The manner in which this battle is resolved sheds yet more light on the relation of human life to the divine in the text.

In the context of Jesus' baptism, holy spirit comes into Jesus (1:10). The presence of holy spirit equips Jesus to cast unclean spirits and demons out of people. On different occasions, these spirit beings call Jesus Holy One of God (1:24) and son of God (3:11; 5:7). Part of being son of God, then, is being equipped with holy spirit in such a manner that one has power over evil, unclean spirits.

When Jesus was in the wilderness forty days immediately after his baptism, angels served him, which means that they fed him (1 Kings 19:5–8). But this is the only time angels are explicitly present in Mark. While other Gospels feature angels at the empty tomb, Mark does not explicitly do so. Some interpreters think the young man in a white robe at the empty tomb is an angel (16:5). If so, this is another implicit rather than explicit reference to something of a divine nature in the text. One might expect angels to come and rescue Jesus from the cross, but they do not. Nor is there reference to holy spirit in the Markan account of the death and resurrection. At the time of Jesus' death, his spirit goes out of him (15:37), but this is a reference to his life-sustaining breath rather than to holy spirit. Spirit beings set the context for powerful activity by Jesus while he is on earth, and conflict between spiritual forces may be implicit in his death. But there is no explicit reference either to holy spirit or to demons in the Markan account of Jesus' death and resurrection. Again, if spirit beings are present in the Markan account of Jesus' death and resurrection, they are present in an implicit, unstated way rather than in an explicit, openly stated way.

D. Divine History

Many sacred texts presuppose that divine powers direct historical processes and events toward certain results. In the New Testament, this is the realm of eschatology, apocalyptic, or salvation history. From the perspective of eschatology, history moves toward the time of "last things." From the perspective of apocalyptic, certain seers see revelations from heaven as the end-time approaches, making events and procedures of the end-time known before they occur. From the perspective of salvation history, God's plan for humans works itself out through a complicated but ever-ongoing process that moves slowly toward God's goals.

While God does not make a vocal reply either to Jesus' request that God remove the ordeal of suffering and death (14:36) or to Jesus' cry that God has forsaken him (15:34), things occur that the reader naturally attributes to the power of God at work in the world. When darkness covers the whole land from the sixth hour until the ninth hour of the day of the crucifixion (15:33), the narration seems to imply that God is the central power and emotion of the universe responding to the death of Jesus. But what kind of response is it? The response seems to imitate the gloom and despair — the dark hour, if you will — in Jesus as he moves through suffering and rejection to death. The response does not include phenomena that hold a promise of restoring Jesus' life, like the earthquake in Matt 27:51–53 that opens the tombs and raises the bodies of many saints who had died. Rather, the cosmos appears to move into death vicariously with Jesus. In other words, the cosmos loses its light — which is the source of life for plants, animals, and humans — at the same time that life is ebbing away from the body of Jesus. When life-giving breath actually goes out of Jesus' body, the curtain of the temple is torn in two from top to bottom (Mark 15:38). In Matt 27:51, the splitting of the curtain occurs in the context of the earthquake that splits the rocks and opens the tombs. But not so in Mark, where the splitting of the temple curtain is the single cosmic phenomenon that occurs when Jesus dies (15:38). Surely the passive form of the verb, "the curtain was split," is a "divine" passive — to be understood as "was split in two from top to bottom by God." In other words, God's action is to be perceived in events that are otherwise unexplained. But both the cause of the event and its meaning are unexplained in Mark. The text leaves the reader with the task of filling in the blanks, so to speak.

As the account continues, the next unexplained event is that the large stone is rolled back when the women come to the tomb after the sabbath. Again the verb is passive with no designation of who rolled it back. The implication again seems to be that God's powers at work in the universe rolled it back. Then the young man at the tomb interprets Jesus' absence as "He has risen" (16:6). In accord with Markan narration, this is not a divine passive, "He has been raised [by God]." Somehow there has been a transformation of Jesus' corpse into a body that could "rise up" out of the tomb. But this transformation, once again, must be the work of God.

In implicit ways in Mark 15:1–16:8, then, God is perceived to be at work. God does not speak in the narrative. But God is perceived as acting, both by what God does and does not do. God does not remove suffering and death from Jesus. Jesus becomes completely alienated from people, and the powers of God in the universe allow him to die. But God responds by giving Jesus' body the power to rise up from death to life. The final implication, then, is that both the death and the resurrection of Jesus are God's will and God's work.

If God is at work in the death and resurrection of Jesus, what kind of divine history is this? Is this part of an overarching process of salvation history that is gradually working toward divine goals? The answer is no. There is not a clear plan of salvation history in Mark. In other words, it is not evident how history might gradually progress over centuries and millennia toward goals the divine has for humans and the world. Rather, events occur during a special eschatological time. Jesus' life, death, and resurrection set the stage for the coming of the Son of man (13:24–26) some time in the near future. Indeed, the kingdom of God will come with power "before some standing here taste death" (9:1).

The death and resurrection of Jesus, therefore, take place in eschatological time. The one explicit hint of this in Mark 15:1–16:8 is that Joseph of Arimathea is looking for the kingdom of God (15:43). Otherwise the eschatological nature of time during the account is implicit. When the chief priests and scribes taunt Jesus as Messiah King of Israel (15:32), the implication is that God's rule has established itself through Jesus as its human agent. But this is part of the mockery by the chief priests and scribes, not a clear characterization of Jesus in the story. In fact, the title Messiah King of Israel seems not to be quite right. As a suffering, dying, and rising son of God, Jesus is significantly different from common perceptions of the Messiah King of Israel.

What kind of eschatological history, then, is this? Why does Jesus have to suffer and die? As we move on to other aspects of the sacred texture of the text, we may find an answer to this question. In this section, however, we observe that Mark presents this history as part of the will of God. Earlier in the story, Jesus tells his disciples, "It is necessary that the Son of man suffer, ... be killed, and after three days rise again" (8:31). The implication is that this will happen simply because God wills it to happen. Jesus also says, "The Son of man goes as it is written of him" (14:21). It is not clear to what scriptural text this might refer, since no text available to us in Hebrew Scripture or the Apocrypha refers to the suffering and death of the Son of man. So far as the Gospel of Mark is concerned, however, "past testimony," which is perceived to be divine information from an earlier time, asserts that the Son of man must suffer and die. From the perspective of Mark, then, this span of history is foreordained to happen in the manner in which it does, and it will come to an end when the Son of man returns on the clouds with the angels in the glory of his father (8:38; 13:26).

E. Human Redemption

Another dimension of sacred texture is the transmission of benefit from the divine to humans as a result of events, rituals, or practices. As a result of things that happen or could happen if people do them, divine powers will transform human lives and take them into a higher level of existence. Perhaps the result will be the changing of the mortal nature of humans — namely, a state of existence that leads to death — into an immortal nature, a state where they will no longer die. Or perhaps a burden of impurity or guilt is removed in such a manner that a person is liberated from powers or practices that are debilitating and destructive.

In Mark 15:1–16:8, the ultimate redeeming moment for Jesus is his rising up. It is not obvious, however, that the transformation of one's body into a body that can rise up from death is meant for all people, or even for all people who believe in Jesus' resurrection. This is a special event that occurs with God's beloved son. What, then, is its benefit for other humans — those who are not specially chosen to be the beloved son of God?

Many times in the narrative, Jesus casts out unclean spirits and demons to restore people to fully functioning human beings. In addition, he heals people by touching them, and some people receive healing when they touch him. Throughout his activity on earth, then, Jesus brings renewal to people whose lives are afflicted. But what happens as a result of his death and resurrection? While Jesus is hanging on the cross, the issue remains the salvation of Jesus himself. People who pass by taunt him to "save himself" by coming down from the cross. Chief priests and scribes assert that he saved others but cannot save himself. So the issue in the account of Jesus' death and resurrection is Jesus' saving of himself rather than his saving of others in some special way through his acceptance of what God wills as a necessity for him.

In Mark 10:45, Jesus tells his disciples that the Son of man has come to serve others and to give his life as a ransom for many. Then in Mark 14:24, Jesus tells his disciples that the cup is his blood of the covenant poured out for many. These two moments bring forth assertions that the purpose of Jesus' death is to bring release from powers of death to other people. Again, however, the fact that this happens and the exact result of its happening remain at an implicit level instead of moving to a level where they are explicitly explained in the story. Once again, exactly what kind of human redemption occurs through Jesus' death and resurrection remains a mystery, hidden except for those who can see it.

F. Human Commitment

The other side of what God and holy persons do for humans is human commitment to divine ways. The sacred texture of a text, therefore, regularly includes a portrayal of humans who are faithful followers and supporters of people who play a special role in revealing the ways of God to humans. In Christian texts, this special form of human commitment is usually called discipleship. In other contexts, it may have other names. In all cases, however, the issue is the response of humans at the level of their practices.

No disciples are present in Mark 15:1–16:8, since they have fled. Three women standing at a distance emerge in the narrative as faithful followers of Jesus through the time of his death. They had followed Jesus from Galilee to Jerusalem, and they had served his needs during that period of time (15:40–41). They do not flee when he is arrested and tried, like the other disciples. Rather, they stay close enough to see what happens to him, and when they see his body laid in a tomb, they make preparations to anoint his body for a proper burial (15:47–16:1). The irony of the story is that when they are told to tell the disciples and Peter that Jesus has risen and is going before them to Galilee, they flee in fright and tell no one (16:6–8). In the end, then, even their commitment is unclear. Interpreters have wrestled with this aspect of Mark, and they differ over their perception of the commitment both of the women and of the disciples of Jesus, all of whom fled at one time or another in relation to Jesus' trial, death, and resurrection. In this instance, however, statements of Jesus earlier in the story make certain dynamics of human commitment a bit clearer than dynamics concerning human redemption. Those who wish to come after Jesus must deny themselves and take up their cross and follow him (8:34). Exactly what their "cross" may be is not evident. Nevertheless, the nature of the commitment is quite clear. It is necessary to commit oneself to an extent that one does not fear death and is willing to do what must be done in a context of a complete threat to one's life. The text undergirds the seriousness of this commitment with the statement by Jesus that, when the Son of man comes in the glory of his father with the holy angels, he will be ashamed of those who are ashamed of him and his words (8:38). In the context of eschatological time, then, the text gives a basic definition of human commitment with certain guidelines.

G. Religious Community

Another aspect of the sacred texture of a text is the formation and nurturing of religious community. In other words, human commitment regularly is not simply an individual matter but a matter of participating with other people in activities that nurture and fulfill commitment to divine ways. In Christian terminology, this is the realm of ecclesiology, which focuses on the assembly of people (ecclesia) called out to worship God and enact obedience to God. Ecclesiology is concerned with the nature of community into which people are called by God. Regularly, primary issues in ecclesiology concern the relation of the community to God, the relation of members of the community to one another, and the commitment of people in the community to people outside it. It is customary for guidelines to be more demanding in terms of forgiveness and acceptance toward people in one's own religious community than to people outside the community. Nevertheless, the community itself customarily has commitments to people in the world outside. Religious community, then, includes commitments to God, to people inside the community, and to people outside the community.

The word *ecclesia*, which translators often translate as "church," occurs in Matthew (16:18; 18:17) but not in Mark. Nevertheless, there are aspects of formation and nurture of religious community in Mark. The presence of the women standing together as a group at a distance implies a common bond among them. Together they buy spices and go to the tomb to anoint his body. This kind of group action is the essence of religious community. In fact, people in Christian communities today repeat this action of going to Jesus' tomb in Jerusalem as a religious ritual that shows commitment to Jesus and to others who identify themselves with the death and resurrection of Jesus. In Mark, we do not see anything that explicitly shows that the women accept responsibility for one another's needs. We also do not see anything that suggests that they do not do this. Again, by implication one might think they would respond to one another's needs in a mode similar to their response to Jesus' needs. But this is another implicit rather than explicit aspect of the sacred texture of Mark.

The statement that Jesus is going before his disciples and Peter to Galilee and that they will see him there (16:7) also implies religious community. The implication is that the disciples represent religious community that has formed around Jesus, and if the disciples would be told what the young man said and would respond to it, they would act together in a mode that further nurtures religious community. The narrative says, of course, that the women did not tell them, because they were afraid. At the end of the account, then, religious community stands as a possibility that the reader does not see fulfilled.

Earlier in the story, Jesus makes the explicit statement that those who do the will of God are his brother, sister, and mother (3:35). Therefore, Jesus uses language of kinship, family relationships, to describe religious community. The narrative shows the will of God for Jesus: it was necessary that Jesus accept suffering, death, and resurrection as the way of being God's beloved son. But what is the will of God for those who participate in religious community associated with Jesus? As mentioned above, Jesus says that his followers must deny themselves, take up their cross, and follow him (8:34). Later in the story, Peter says that he and his fellow disciples have left everything and followed Jesus (10:28). Jesus enumerates the things they have left: house, brothers, sisters, mother, father, children, and lands (10:29). Does this mean that all people must leave these things to be people who do the will of God? Again these things are implicit rather than explicit in Mark. One might think this is a special requirement for people who dedicate their lives to a special form of service that members of the religious community support. In other words, the other side of religious community may be implicit in Jesus' further statement that those who have left everything will receive "a hundredfold in this time houses, brothers, sisters, mothers, and lands, with persecutions, and in the age to come eternal life" (10:30). Members of the religious community who have not accepted the special tasks of traveling around provide hospitality, generosity according to the traveler's needs, and food and wealth from the land. This is another aspect of the sacred texture of Mark that remains at an implicit level. Certain guidelines do appear, however, and they call people into religious community in relation to the life, death, and resurrection of Jesus.

H. Ethics

Ethics concerns the responsibility of humans to think and act in special ways in both ordinary and extraordinary circumstances. When addressed in the context of religious commitment, the special ways of thinking and acting are motivated by commitment to God. Usually, ethicists work in some way with ethical principles, though some consider ethical guidelines, rules, or principles to be so intrinsic to situations that they cannot be adequately stated. While for some decades during the twentieth century many interpreters have not considered it possible to develop a New Testament ethics, a number of interpreters now think such an ethics should be possible to formulate.

In the Gospel of Mark, perhaps the closest thing to an ethical principle is the assertion of Jesus that those who seek to save their life will lose it and those who lose their life for the sake of Jesus and the gospel will save it (8:35). Intrinsic to this is a conviction that humans are not able to grasp and secure divine benefits for their own lives. In other words, divine benefits must come from the divine through divine ways. Mark 15:1–16:8 appears to be a narrative presentation of the manner in which Jesus embodied this principle. He himself did not seek to save his life, and through the process of losing his life, his life was restored to him by God. The process is mysterious, and the end result is mysterious. In other words, it is not clear just what life is like once it is "saved," but it quite clearly means something that happens through a total commitment of life to God's ways. Being saved is not something that happens while a person is still on earth. Rather, it is something that is given in the context of the end of one's life.

The ethical dimension of saving one's life by losing it requires that one be willing to do things that threaten one's life if those things fulfill the will of God. But what things are the will of God? The narrative shows what kinds of things they are. They are not things like killing other people. They are not even things like judging other people. Rather, they are things like accepting tasks and responsibilities that offer benefits to others and that affirm the importance and life of people who are otherwise excluded from the benefits of society.

From the perspective of ethics, one of the most interesting people in Mark 15:1–16:8 in addition to Jesus is Joseph of Arimathea. The implication of the narrative is that, as a member of the council, he participated in the decision that Jesus was guilty and deserved death (14:64; 15:43). Though other people with official status in relation to the temple speak against Jesus and mock him during his crucifixion, Joseph has the courage to request the body of Jesus and give it a proper burial (15:43–46). Why would he do such a thing? The narrator tells us that he was looking for the kingdom of God (15:43). This evidently means that he had a commitment to the will of God that motivated him to do a right and honorable thing, even though there may have been danger in it. At the heart of his action, then, may be an ethical commitment to the will of God that expresses itself in offering benefit to others even in circumstances that threaten one's reputation or even one's life. In a context where no one else acts, he is the one who, though he is supposed to be on the side of Jesus' adversaries, requests the body of Jesus and gives it an honorable burial. There may, then, be moments in the Gospel of Mark that provide data for ethics.

Conclusion

The sacred texture of a text, then, includes aspects concerning deity, holy persons, spirit beings, divine history, human redemption, human commitment, religious community, and ethics. These aspects of a text are embedded deeply in the inner texture, intertexture, social and cultural texture, and ideological texture of a text. For this reason, a major way to gain a fuller understanding of the meanings and meaning-effects of sacred texture is through analysis and interpretation of other textures in the context of an understanding of its sacred texture. Some people begin and end their analyses of biblical texts with analysis of their sacred texture. The result is a disembodiment of their sacred texture from the realities of living in the world. As an interpreter works carefully with the nature of language itself in a text, with the relation of a text to other texts, and with the material, social, cultural, and ideological nature of life, a thick description of the sacred texture of a text emerges. This description is truer to the rich complexity of a sacred text than exploration that limits itself to only one texture of the text.

Much of the sacred texture of the Gospel of Mark emerges through implicit aspects of the text. In other words, many aspects of the relation of human life to the divine are not given open, direct, and explicit expression. Aspects of the sacred texture of Mark, in fact, may be not only mysterious or secret but paradoxical. Mark 4:11–12 asserts that Jesus gives the secret or mystery of the kingdom of God to his disciples, but to everyone outside everything happens in parables. Perhaps interpreters experience something like this when they programmatically explore the sacred texture of the Gospel of Mark. In the end, the disciples who were given the secret of the kingdom seemed not to understand what was happening in the rejection, suffering, and death of Jesus. Perhaps we do not understand either. But perhaps we experience the phenomena of the text in such a way that they function as parables that are not simply riddles but are little dramas about life in the world when one is committed to ways of the divine.

Conclusion

Socio-rhetorical criticism, then, challenges interpreters to explore a text in a systematic, broad manner that leads to a rich environment of interpretation and dialogue. Underlying the method is a presupposition that words themselves work in very complicated ways to communicate meanings that we only partially understand. It also presupposes that meanings themselves have their meanings by their relation to other meanings. In other words, all of our attempts to name truth are very limited insights into small aspects of the relation of things and meanings to one another. Interpreters and investigators have acquired amazing abilities, however, to describe the relation of things and meanings in complex but structured ways that are highly informative about life and the world in which we live. Socio-rhetorical criticism challenges interpreters to use these amazing human abilities when they investigate and interpret biblical texts.

While analyses of inner texture, intertexture, social and cultural texture, and sacred texture are widely accepted as serious scholarly ventures, some interpreters do not want to talk about ideology in interpretation because they fear interpretation will become "simply" ideology. It will be obvious to the reader that I do not share this view. I hope the reader understands why I do not share this view. I think there are all kinds of phenomena in texts that invite systematic, programmatic analysis that approaches "scientific" activity. Analysis in these arenas of a text can reach a state of sophistication whereby students and scholars can enter into serious "scientific" assessment of the strengths and weaknesses of various assertions. This does not mean that interpreters of a text have the same opportunity that scientists have to repeat experiments in laboratories in such a manner that they can establish the approximation of certain theories to testable "natural" processes. It does mean that phenomena reside in texts in a manner that makes them programmatically and systematically analyzable, even though all the time the interpreters are deeply invested ideologically. For me, this is enough. Even though texts are ideological constructions, they are not "only" ideological constructions. They are sites that invite us to use multiple skills of memory, reasoning, playing, working, hoping, feeling.... I invite you to fill in the blanks.

Bibliography

Adam, A. K. H. 1995. *What Is Post-Modern Criticism?* Minneapolis: Fortress Press.

Bailey, James L., and Lyle D. Vander Broek. 1992. *Literary Forms in the New Testament: A Handbook.* Louisville, Ky.: Westminster/John Knox Press.

Barth, Fredrik. 1969. Introduction to *Ethnic Groups and Boundaries,* edited by F. Barth. Boston: Little, Brown and Co. Also published as "Ethnic Groups and Boundaries." In *Process and Form in Social Life,* by F. Barth, 198–227. London: Routledge and Kegan Paul, 1981.

Berger, Peter, and Thomas Luckmann. 1967. *The Social Construction of Reality: A Treatise in the Sociology of Knowledge.* Garden City, N.Y.: Doubleday.

Bhabha, Homi K. 1992. "Postcolonial Criticism." In *Redrawing the Boundaries: The Transformation of English and Literary Studies,* edited by Stephen Greenblatt and Giles Gunn. New York: Modern Language Association of America, 437–65.

Blount, Brian K. 1993. "A Socio-Rhetorical Analysis of Simon of Cyrene: Mark 15:21 and Its Parallels." *Semeia* 63:171–98.

Boissevain, Jeremy. 1974. *Friends of Friends: Networks, Manipulators and Coalitions.* Oxford: Basil Blackwell.

Bouvard, Margarite. 1975. *The Intentional Community Movement: Building a New Moral World.* Port Washington, N.Y.: Kennikat.

Burke, Kenneth. 1931. *Counter-Statement.* Berkeley: University of California Press.

Carney, Thomas F. 1975. *The Shape of the Past: Models and Antiquity.* Lawrence, Kans.: Coronado Press.

Castelli, Elizabeth A. 1991. *Imitating Paul: A Discourse of Power.* Louisville, Ky.: Westminster/John Knox Press.

Chatman, Seymour. 1978. *Story and Discourse: Narrative Structure in Fiction and Film.* Ithaca, N.Y.: Cornell University Press.

Conzelman, Hans. 1987. *The Acts of the Apostles.* Translated by J. Limburg, A. T. Kraabel, and D. H. Juel. Hermeneia. Philadelphia: Fortress Press.

Dahl, Nils A. 1974. "Nations in the New Testament." In *New Testament Christianity for Africa and the World: Essays in Honor of Harry Sawyer,* edited by Mark E. Glaswell and E. Fashole-Luke. London: SPCK, 54–68.

Davis, David Brion. 1975. *The Problem of Slavery in the Age of Revolution 1770–1823.* Ithaca, N.Y.: Cornell University Press.

Dean-Otting, Miriam, and Vernon K. Robbins. 1993. "Biblical Sources for Pronouncement Stories in the Gospels." *Semeia* 63:93–113.

Dio Chrysostom. 1971. *I. Discourses I–IX.* Translated by J. W. Cohoon. Loeb Classical Library. Cambridge, Mass.: Harvard University Press.

Donahue, John R. 1988. "Mark." In *Harper's Bible Commentary,* edited by James L. Mays. San Francisco: Harper and Row.

Douglas, Mary. 1966. *Purity and Danger: An Analysis of Concepts of Pollution and Taboo.* London: Routledge and Kegan Paul.

Dreyfus, Hubert L., and Paul Rabinow. 1983. *Michel Foucault: Beyond Structuralism and Hermeneutics.* Chicago: University of Chicago Press.

Eagleton, T. 1991. *Ideology: An Introduction.* London: Verso Press.

Ellens, G. F. S. 1971. "The Ranting Ranters: Reflections on a Ranting Counter-Culture." *Church History* 40:91–107.

Elliott, John H. 1990. *A Home for the Homeless: A Social-Scientific Criticism of 1 Peter, Its Situation and Strategy.* Reprint, paperback edition with new introduction. Philadelphia: Fortress Press.

———. 1993. *What Is Social-Scientific Criticism?* Minneapolis: Fortress Press.

———, ed. 1986. *Social-Scientific Criticism of the New Testament and Its Social World.* Vol. 35 of *Semeia.* Decatur, Ga.: Scholars Press.

Gager, John G. 1975. *Kingdom and Community: The Social World of Early Christianity.* Englewood Cliffs, N.J.: Prentice-Hall.

Gealy, F. D. 1962. "Ethiopian Eunuch." In *Interpreter's Dictionary of the Bible,* edited by George A. Buttrick. Nashville: Abingdon Press, 1:177–78.

Gordon, Milton M. 1970. "The Subsociety and the Subculture." In *Subcultures,* edited by D. Arnold. Berkeley, Calif.: Glendessary Press, 150–63.

Goudriaan, Koen. 1992. "Ethnical Strategies in Graeco-Roman Egypt." In *Ethnicity in Hellenistic Egypt,* edited by Per Bilde et al. Aarhus: Aarhus University Press, 74–99.

Hengel, Martin. 1977. *Crucifixion in the Ancient World and the Folly of the Message of the Cross.* Philadelphia: Fortress Press.

Hock, Ronald F., and Edward N. O'Neil. 1986. *The Chreia in Ancient Rhetoric.* Vol. 1: *The Progymnasmata.* Atlanta: Scholars Press.

Johnson, Luke Timothy. 1992. *The Acts of the Apostles.* Sacra Pagina 5. Collegeville, Minn.: Liturgical Press.

Kaibel, G. 1889. *Comicorum Graecorum Fragmenta.* Berlin.

Kennedy, George A. 1984. *New Testament Interpretation through Rhetorical Criticism.* Chapel Hill: University of North Carolina Press.

Kloppenborg, John S. 1988. *Q Parallels: Synopsis, Critical Notes and Concordance.* Sonoma, Calif.: Polebridge Press.

Lane, William L. 1974. *The Gospel according to Mark.* Grand Rapids: William B. Eerdmans.

Mack, Burton L. 1988. *A Myth of Innocence: Mark and Christian Origins.* Philadelphia: Fortress Press.

———. 1990. *Rhetoric and the New Testament.* Minneapolis: Fortress Press.

———. 1993. *The Lost Gospel: The Book of Q and Christian Origins.* San Francisco: HarperSanFrancisco.

Mack, Burton L., and Vernon K. Robbins. 1989. *Patterns of Persuasion in the Gospels.* Sonoma, Calif.: Polebridge Press.

Mair, Lucy. 1965. *An Introduction to Social Anthropology.* Oxford: Clarendon Press.

Malherbe, Abraham. 1987. *Paul and the Thessalonians: The Philosophic Tradition of Pastoral Care.* Philadelphia: Fortress Press.

———. 1989. *Paul and the Popular Philosophers.* Philadelphia: Fortress.

———. 1995. "Determinism and Free Will in Paul: The Argument of 1 Corinthians 8 and 9." In *Paul in His Hellenistic Context*, edited by Troels Engberg-Pedersen. Minneapolis: Fortress Press, 231–55.

Malina, Bruce J. 1993. *The New Testament World: Insights from Cultural Anthropology*. Rev. ed. Atlanta: John Knox Press.

Malina, Bruce J., and Richard L. Rohrbaugh. 1992. *Social-Science Commentary on the Synoptic Gospels*. Minneapolis: Fortress Press.

Marcus, Joel. 1992. *The Way of the Lord: Christological Exegesis of the Old Testament in the Gospel of Mark*. Louisville, Ky.: Westminster/John Knox Press.

Martin, Clarice J. 1989. "A Chamberlain's Journey and the Challenge of Interpretation for Liberation." *Semeia* 47:105–35. Reprinted in *The Bible and Liberation: Political and Social Hermeneutics*, edited by Norman K. Gottward and Richard A. Horsley. Rev. ed. Maryknoll, N.Y.: Orbis Books, 1993.

Martyn, J. Louis. 1968. *History and Theology in the Fourth Gospel*. New York: Harper and Row.

Matera, Frank J. 1986. *Passion Narratives and Gospel Theologies: Interpreting the Synoptics through Their Passion Stories*. New York: Paulist Press.

Merritt, H. Wayne. 1993. *In Word and Deed: Moral Integrity in Paul*. Emory Studies in Early Christianity. New York: Peter Lang.

Merritt, Robert L. 1985. "Jesus, Barabbas, and the Paschal Pardon." *Journal of Biblical Literature* 104:57–68.

Moore, Stephen D. 1992. *Mark and Luke in Poststructuralist Perspectives: Jesus Begins to Write*. New Haven: Yale University Press.

———. 1994 *Poststructuralism and the New Testament: Derrida and Foucault at the Foot of the Cross*. Minneapolis: Fortress Press.

Myers, Ched. 1988. *Binding the Strong Man: A Political Reading of Mark's Story of Jesus*. Maryknoll, N.Y.: Orbis Books.

Neyrey, Jerome H. 1993. *2 Peter, Jude*. Anchor Bible. Vol. 37C. New York: Doubleday.

———, ed. 1991. *The Social World of Luke-Acts: Models for Interpretation*. Peabody, Mass.: Hendrickson Publishers.

Niebuhr, H. Richard. 1951. *Christ and Culture*. New York: Harper and Row.

Østergård, Uffe. 1992. "What Is National and Ethnic Identity?" In *Ethnicity in Hellenistic Egypt*, edited by Per Bilde et al. Aarhus: Aarhus University Press, 16–38.

Petersen, Norman R. 1978. *Literary Criticism for New Testament Critics*. Philadelphia: Fortress Press.

Pitt-Rivers, Julian. 1968. "The Stranger, the Guest and the Hostile Host: Introduction to the Study of the Laws of Hospitality." In *Contributions to Mediterranean Sociology*, edited by J. G. Peristiany. Paris: Mouton, 12–30.

Potter, Jack M., May N. Diaz, and George M. Foster, eds. 1967. *Peasant Society: A Reader*. Boston: Little, Brown and Co.

Powell, Mark Allan. 1990. *What Is Narrative Criticism?* Minneapolis: Fortress Press.

Rhetorica ad Herennium. [Cicero]. 1954. *Ad C. Herennium*. Translated by Harry Caplan. Loeb Classical Library. Cambridge, Mass.: Harvard University Press.

Robbins, Vernon K. 1981. "Summons and Outline in Mark: The Three-Step Progression." *Novum Testamentum* 23:97–114. Reprinted in Robbins 1994b:119–35.

————. 1988a. "The Chreia." In *Greco-Roman Literature and the New Testament*, edited by David E. Aune. Atlanta: Scholars Press, 1–23.

————. 1988b. "The Crucifixion and the Speech of Jesus." *Forum* 4/1:33–46.

————. 1991a. "The Social Location of the Implied Author of Luke-Acts." In Neyrey 1991:305–32.

————. 1991b. "Writing as a Rhetorical Act in Plutarch and the Gospels." In *Persuasive Artistry: Studies in New Testament Rhetoric in Honor of George A. Kennedy*, edited by Duane F. Watson. Sheffield: JSOT Press, 157–86.

————. 1992a. *Jesus the Teacher: A Socio-Rhetorical Interpretation of Mark.* Reprinted paperback edition with new introduction and additional indexes. Minneapolis: Fortress Press. Originally published, 1984.

————. 1992b. "The Reversed Contextualization of Psalm 22 in the Markan Crucifixion: A Socio-Rhetorical Analysis." In *The Four Gospels 1992: Festschrift Frans Neirynck*, edited by F. Van Segbroeck et al. Bibliotheca ephemeridum theologicarum lovaniensium 100. Louvain: Leuven University Press, 2:1161–83.

————. 1992c. "Using a Socio-Rhetorical Poetics to Develop a Unified Method: The Woman Who Anointed Jesus as a Test Case." In *Society of Biblical Literature Seminar Papers:* 302–19.

————. 1993a. "Progymnastic Rhetorical Composition and Pre-gospel Traditions: A New Approach." In *The Synoptic Gospels: Source Criticism and the New Literary Criticism*, edited by Camille Focant. Bibliotheca ephemeridum theologicarum lovaniensium 110. Louvain: Leuven University Press, 111–47.

————. 1993b. "Rhetoric and Culture: Exploring Types of Cultural Rhetoric in a Text." In *Rhetoric and the New Testament: Essays from the (1992) Heidelberg Conference*, edited by Stanley E. Porter and Thomas H. Olbricht. Sheffield: Sheffield Academic Press, 447–67.

————, ed. 1993c. *The Rhetoric of Pronouncement.* Vol. 64 of *Semeia*. Atlanta: Scholars Press.

————. 1994a. "Interpreting Miracle Culture and Parable Culture in Mark 4–11." *Svensk Exegetisk Årsbok* 59:59–81.

————. 1994b. *New Boundaries in Old Territory: Forms and Social Rhetoric in Mark.* New York: Peter Lang.

————. 1994c. "Oral, Rhetorical, and Literary Cultures: A Response." *Semeia* 65:75–91.

————. 1994d. "Socio-Rhetorical Criticism: Mary, Elizabeth, and the Magnificat as a Test Case." In *The New Literary Criticism and the New Testament*, edited by Elizabeth Struthers Malbon and Edgar V. McKnight. Sheffield: Sheffield Academic Press, 164–209.

————. 1995a. "Divine Dialogue and the Lord's Prayer: Socio-Rhetorical Interpretation of Sacred Texts." *Dialogue* 28:117–46.

————. 1995b. "Social-Scientific Criticism and Literary Studies: Prospects for Cooperation in Biblical Interpretation." In *Modelling Early Christianity: Social-Scientific Studies of the New Testament in Its Context*, edited by Philip F. Esler. London: Routledge, 274–89.

————. 1996. *The Tapestry of Early Christian Discourse: Rhetoric, Society and Ideology.* London: Routledge.

Roberts, Keith A. 1978. "Toward a Generic Concept of Counter-Culture." *Sociological Focus* 11:111–26.

Schneiders, Sandra M. 1991. *The Revelatory Text: Interpreting the New Testament as Scripture.* San Francisco: HarperSanFrancisco.

Schürer, Emil. 1973. *The History of the Jewish People in the Age of Jesus Christ (175 B.C.–A.D. 135),* edited by G. Vermes et al. Rev. ed. Edinburgh: T. and T. Clark.

Smith, Jonathan Z. 1978. *Map Is Not Territory: Studies in the History of Religions.* Chicago: University of Chicago Press.

Snowden, Frank M. 1976a. "Ethiopians in the Greco-Roman World." In *The African Diaspora: Interpretive Essays,* edited by Martin L. Kilson and Robert I. Rottbert. Cambridge, Mass.: Harvard University Press, 11–36.

———. 1976b. "Iconographical Evidence on the Black Populations in Greco-Roman Antiquity." In *The Image of the Black in Western Art: From the Pharaoh to the Fall of the Roman Empire,* edited by Ladislas Bugner. New York: William Morrow, 1:133–245.

———. 1979. *Blacks in Antiquity: Ethiopians in the Greco-Roman Experience.* Cambridge, Mass.: Harvard University Press.

Stark, Werner. 1967. *Sectarian Religion.* New York: Fordham University Press.

Taylor, Vincent. 1963. *The Gospel according to St. Mark.* London: Macmillan.

Thomas, Brook. 1991. *The New Historicism and Other Old-fashioned Topics.* Princeton, N.J.: Princeton University Press.

Tolbert, Mary Ann. 1992. "Mark." In *The Women's Bible Commentary,* edited by Carol A. Newsom and Sharon H. Ringe. Louisville, Ky.: Westminster/John Knox Press.

Van Iersel, Bas. 1989. *Reading Mark.* Translated by W. H. Bisscheroux. Edinburgh: T. and T. Clark.

Vardaman, J. 1962. "A New Inscription Which Mentions Pilate as 'Prefect.'" *Journal of Biblical Literature* 81:70–71.

Veeser, H. Aram, ed. 1989. *The New Historicism.* New York: Routledge.

Watson, Duane F. 1993. "Paul's Rhetorical Strategy in 1 Corinthians 15." In *Rhetoric and the New Testament: Essays from the 1992 Heidelberg Conference,* edited by Stanley E. Porter and Thomas H. Olbricht. Sheffield: Sheffield Academic Press, 231–49.

Watson, Duane F., and Alan J. Hauser. 1994. *Rhetorical Criticism of the Bible: A Comprehensive Bibliography with Notes on History and Method.* Biblical Interpretation Series 4. Leiden: Brill.

Wilde, James A. 1978. "The Social World of Mark's Gospel: A Word about Method." In *Society of Biblical Literature Seminar Papers* 2:47–67.

Wilson, Bryan R. 1963. "A Typology of Sects in a Dynamic and Comparative Perspective." *Archives de Sociologie de Religion* 16:49–63.

———. 1969. "A Typology of Sects." In *Sociology of Religion,* edited by Roland Robertson. Baltimore: Penguin Books, 361–83.

———. 1973. *Magic and the Millennium: A Sociological Study of Religious Movements of Protest among Tribal and Third-World Peoples.* New York: Harper and Row.

Wolf, E. R. 1966. *Peasants.* Englewood Cliffs, N.J.: Prentice-Hall.

Wordelman, Amy L. 1993. "The Gods Have Come Down: Images of Historical Lycaonia and the Literary Construction of Acts 14." Ph.D. dissertation, Princeton University.

Wuthnow, Robert. 1992. "Infrastructure and Superstructure: Revisions in Marxist Sociology of Culture." In *Theory of Culture*, edited by Richard Münch and Neil J. Smelser. Berkeley: University of California Press, 145–70.

Yinger, J. Milton. 1960. "Contraculture and Subculture." *American Sociological Review* 25:625–35.

———. 1982. *Countercultures: The Promise and the Peril of a World Turned Upside Down*. New York: Free Press.

Index of Scriptures
and Ancient Texts

Index of Modern Authors

Index of Subjects